Linked Outbound

Build Your Sales Pipeline with
Social Selling and Sales Navigator™

by Sam Rathling

1st Edition (May 2023)

Contents

Dedicated to my 3 amazing children
Oscar, Maya and Liliana who are my inspiration
and my world. I love you all to the moon and
back, a million times. Mum xxx

Foreword

by Nicholas Jones

CEO, Entrepreneur & Business Mentor

Before starting to work with Sam in 2018, I had never heard of LinkedIn. Our companies always used the traditional approach to selling. Reps on the ground, cold calling and hard graft. I was sceptical when she first told me that it could transform the way we work.

Fast Forward to today and everything has changed. Not only have Sam, Chris and I built one of the most well-recognised LinkedIn and Social Marketing companies in the world, we're also utilising Sam's Social Selling methodologies across all our sales and marketing operations, with huge success.

Sales is still not easy, but with the right application of Social Selling, the ability of our organisations to find, nurture and close business both from within our existing accounts and our untapped target market.

This book is a must read for sales leaders, sales professionals, BDRs, SDMs, Marketing Managers and all those involved in the process of business acquisition.

You won't regret it!

Nick

Introduction:
Why I Wrote This Book

This book was written for every frustrated sales leader, every hard-working business owner and every dedicated sales and marketing professional who struggles to fill their sales pipeline with qualified opportunities on a consistent basis.

I've been on a mission to help organisations with social selling for over a decade and it baffles me the amount of money that companies throw at marketing and sales strategies that just don't work!

I wrote this book to showcase the huge opportunity that is within the reach of every company on the planet, regardless of their industry, headcount, age or turnover. Social selling can be done for little or low investment, and when done well can:

4

- Position your business as the 'go-to' brand in your industry
- Provide a steady flow of leads into your business
- Help your sales team to own their personal brand, building pipeline
- Build brand awareness and visibility of your products and services
- Align your sales and marketing teams, no more blame game
- Give you a massive competitive advantage
- Help you to keep and retain existing clients
- Open opportunities to secure key accounts and drive logo acquisition
- Attract 'A players' into your business, so you recruit the best
- Position your Leaders as the industry thought leaders that they are
- Start conversations with your IDEAL clients
- Proactively target the right people in key accounts, outbound leads
- Attract new customers, with inbound leads

This book will focus on the OUTBOUND aspects mentioned above. I will touch on the inbound strategies too, but if you have not already read the accompanying "Linked Inbound" then that would be a good book to read alongside this one.

There are essentially two ways to get business from social selling, inbound and outbound leads (more on that in the first chapter). The reason I wrote this book is that so many people focus on content creation and building their personal brand and think that this will be enough to get them business, but for most simply putting content out there is not enough to create a sustainable pipeline.

When I go into organisations and work with sales and marketing teams, it's usually because the company has invested heavily in Sales Navigator™ licenses but their salespeople are not generating enough leads. The leadership team has high expectations and expect that their salesforce will magically start producing new opportunities from LinkedIn®, because they gave them a Sales Navigator™ licence. Unfortunately, it's not a magic wand!

Social selling is a marathon, not a sprint. Most people are looking for instant gratification, a quick fix and don't understand that building a personal brand and building a sustainable sales pipeline takes time. Without proper training on how to prospect and outreach to decision makers, how to build the successful habits that create leads and how to stand out and not look and act like every other salesperson on LinkedIn®, most will fail and give up.

I wrote this book to help support you and your team. If you are a business owner, without a sales team or you are reading this and don't currently have Sales Navigator™, you will still get value from this book. You may even decide after reading this that you will make that investment. Either way my goal here is to help you proactively create opportunities for your business that help you to win more business.

The last thing to say before we get into the detail, is that I am independent. I don't work for LinkedIn®, I never have, but I am a HUGE fan of their platform. I have built several companies utilising what I am going to share with you here in this book, I am a Chief Revenue Officer myself, in our company we follow everything in this book to the letter. At Pipeline 44, we book meetings every week with mid-size and enterprise level companies that have sales teams because of the outbound strategies you are going to unlock here. We drive over 500 registrations a month to our free online workshops that help individuals and small business owners with their LinkedIn® efforts using one of the prospecting methods I am going to share with you in the book.

I have invested over 30,000 hours in the LinkedIn® platform and have worked with Sales Navigator™ since its launch in 2014. Everything I am going to share with you is tried and tested, we do this for our own business, as well as our agency and corporate clients, who come to us for help with their prospecting and content on LinkedIn®.

My hope is that you find this book insightful, useful, and full of practical tips. I love reading books that give me actionable take-aways so that's how I write. It's conversational and practical. Each chapter has 5 actions you can do to implement what you are learning as you go.

Enjoy!

Chapter 1:
Your Sales Pipeline

There are two ways to generate business from LinkedIn®. Your leads will either come inbound, where the person messages you saying something along the lines of "I've been following your content, can we book a call?". Or outbound, where you created the opportunity by starting a conversation through an outreach message. Inbound is my favourite kind and, I am fortunate to be in a position where inbound leads happen on a daily basis for me and my team.

How nice would it be to have prospects messaging you, on a regular basis asking if they can book a call or meet you to discuss business. I get it, you probably aren't there right now, but over time you can get there by following some simple steps and creating daily and weekly habits that set you up for success, more on that in Chapter 22.

The simple distinction between inbound and outbound is:

Inbound = Reactive

Outbound = Proactive

Inbound can be sporadic, unpredictable, and inconsistent. You can't rely only on inbound leads, especially if the inbound is not coming from your ideal target market. I have 4 different tiers of target market. Do we get leads from all of them? Yes. Do we get enough inbound leads to reach our stretch sales targets? No. So that means, that despite having a steady flow of inbound leads, we don't want to rely on them, due to me having no control over where they are coming from, who in each of the organisations is reaching out to me, and why they want to speak to me.

Inbound also takes a long time, especially if you are starting with a small network. If you have less than 5000 followers on LinkedIn® then posting content is a key part of your strategy, but don't expect to start getting inbound enquiries for at least 9-12 months. Posting consistency is key, but also the quality of what you are posting needs to be good, more on that in a later chapter.

If you already have more than 5000 followers but you currently post inconsistently (less than twice a week) or you never post original content on the newsfeed, you just share other people's content, then don't expect to be getting inbound enquiries. The content you put out there is about creating awareness, building credibility, and driving up your visibility which over time will turn into business, but in months and years from now, not today or next week.

Outbound is the only way that you can gain control, and proactively create enough opportunities to achieve your sales quota. Outbound, when done consistently and the right way is one of the best ways to build a sustainable sales pipeline. You can control who you are targeting, what job titles you are reaching out to, the size of business you are prospecting, in the relevant and appropriate industry and/or location, that matches your exact target market.

Outbound starts conversations, creates opportunities and allows you to open the door to opportunities that simply wouldn't come your way from solely relying on content. If you work in sales or run sales team, outbound prospecting whether that is through LinkedIn® or picking up the phone and cold-calling, or a combination of both (recommended), is by far the most effective way to generate business.

If you are in marketing and buying data or lists and feeding them to your sales team, stop. These are usually expensive, out of date and don't give you the names of people to speak to. LinkedIn is a live database of ready-made data, waiting to be mined. Sales Navigator™ in my opinion is one of the best sales tools available and I will go into great detail in this book on how you can leverage it.

If you are running your own business and/or are just beginning your entrepreneurial journey, and don't have a sales team yet, then the outbound starts with you. Outbound prospecting no matter how busy you are, should be a key part of your sales strategy. The problem is that most people don't have the time, don't know where to start, don't know what to say and in many cases have a lot of fear about reaching out to complete strangers. Sound familiar?

Before we get started on how to drive more outbound leads, it's important that you understand the fundamentals of pipeline building, which is what this entire book is designed to help you do.

What is a Pipeline?

A sales pipeline is an organised way of tracking potential buyers as they progress through different stages in the buying process. Often, pipelines are visualised as a horizontal bar, sometimes as a funnel, divided into the various stages of a company's sales process. Leads and prospects are moved from one stage to the next as they move through the sales process.

It is a powerful tool for sales managers and business owners, to enable critical decision making. Knowing exactly where each prospect is in your sales pipeline, helps you to forecast, which can help you make decisions on hiring, spending, cost reduction, resource allocation and more.

With a pipeline that is properly up to date and accurate, you can see exactly where your deals and other sales efforts are at all times. This is vital, given that business owners and salespeople are often juggling many leads, prospects and deals and can't afford to let anything slip through the cracks.

As well as providing accountability, a sales pipeline also offers visibility into which sales activities are giving your company the greatest return. It's a tool that can make a significant difference to your bottom line. The different stages of a pipeline can help you visualise your sales process so you can where in the sales funnel your prospects are, which ones are stalling, and which activities are contributing to revenue. If you aren't using a sales pipeline, you may lack valuable insights about how effective your sales process is.

What are the Stages of a Pipeline?

Every company is different, and you may have your own version of these stages. I am going to share the various pipeline stages we use at the Pipeline 44 Group in our own business, and with our clients to help explain, so that if this is not something you currently work with, you can get an idea of how yours might look.

New Lead (1%)
This could come from anywhere, your website, a lead magnet, a message on LinkedIn, a referral, an email into your sales inbox, other social media, a networking event. It's the first expression of interest in what you have to offer. The chances of most of these turning into a client are low, but you want lots of these. Your pipeline should be packed full of new leads.

Nurture (10%)
These are leads that are not close to buying anything. They need more time; they are not currently in the buying window. They need to see more from, more social proof that you are the right solution for them. They are just not ready, and although they may buy in the future, it won't be happening now. Think of these as ones to keep 'warm'. There are many ways to nurture leads and some of that can be done through social selling, which I will get to later. It is advisable to have other sales cadences in place to nurture, for example keeping them on your email list.

Qualification (20%)
This is the discovery phase, for most business owners and salespeople this may include one, two or even three meetings. Pain discovery, understanding the client, understanding their needs, seeing if you can help. The less selling you do in this phase the better. Ask great questions to establish if they have a pain you can fix now or in the future. It may take multiple meetings depending on the size of the opportunity. The larger the deal size the longer the sales cycle and there will be more people involved in the decision. You are either going to qualify them IN and move them to the next stage in the pipeline or qualify them OUT (disqualification – more on that shortly).

Qualified Prospect (40%)

They have a pain you can fix, the right person in the business you are selling to is both willing and able to make a buying decision, there are no red flags. You have chosen to qualify them in, not disqualify them out. They are a match to your IDEAL client (more on that in the next chapter) and you want to move them up the pipeline.

Order Expected (60%)

At this point in the sales process, you are fairly confident that this deal is going to close. In fact, we don't move anything to 60% unless we are sure, as this automatically moves this prospect into our forecast, upon which we make decisions. Order expected should only be used if you actually expect it to close.

Order Confirmation (95%)

The prospect has agreed to the deal, they have verbally confirmed or told you in writing they want to proceed. Too many people jump the gun here and consider this stage to be a sale. It is not. You have only made a sale once you have a signed contract or purchase order.

Order (100%)

Congratulations! The customer has placed a valid purchase order (PO) or signed a contract for your products or services. Only once you have contract signed or a PO is the deal closed. It should not be considered closed until this point.

Lost (0%)

It is important that you track these. You lost the deal. Why? Record it. There could be all sorts of reasons that a deal is lost. Understand the reasons.

Disqualified (0%)

The most successful salespeople I know, focus more on disqualification than anything else. Some prospects will fall out of your sales pipeline because you chose not to continue to sell to them. Despite wanting to buy from you, some prospects just aren't a good fit.

At Pipeline 44, we have a checklist of 15 criteria that a client must meet before starting to work with our agency. If they don't meet all 15, we disqualify them, or we send the client off to do the work until they meet the qualification criteria.

We also have non-negotiable red flags. If they have any one of our red flags, they are disqualified. We know that either they aren't willing to put in the work or don't align with our values and would end up being too high maintenance, sucking the resources in our team. We don't sell all costs; we don't close everyone. Our agency clients must get through quite a few hoops in order to work with us. So, we disqualify heavily.

If this concept is new to you, it should give you a helpful guide. If you already have specific pipeline stages great. We match our pipeline stages to our CRM and our management team gets sales reports each month based on the pipeline. Anything above 60% is reported on in the sales forecast and every deal has a prognosis date attached to it, telling us when that deal is expected to close.

Knowing your numbers is critical to any outbound strategy, so we are going to look at that next.

Know Your Numbers

When it comes to pipeline here are some numbers you MUST know if you want to understand your pipeline and get to grips with how many leads you need to meet your sales targets.

- What is your sales target for each month, quarter and financial year?
- How many new customers do you need to meet those targets?
- How many leads do you need to secure a meeting?
- How many 1st meetings do you need to secure a sale?
- How many 2nd or 3rd meetings do you need to close bigger deals?
- How many meetings in total to close a deal by product/offering?
- How long is your average sales cycle by product/offering?
- What is your average order value by product/offering?
- What is your conversion rate on referrals?
- What is your conversion rate on cold leads?

Let's walk through an example. This is hypothetical but is based on one of the offerings at Pipeline 44. We have 4 different target markets and 6 different service offerings.

This hypothetical example is based on our service 'Content Pro' for our content agency, where clients work with us on a 'done with you' basis. We write content for them in their tone of voice and educate them on all aspects of social selling whilst they are in our ecosystem.

Annual Target Sales Revenue: £500,000
Average Order Value: £ 11,520
Total New Customers needed: 44 (rounded up)
Lead:Meeting Ratio: 3:1 (From 3 leads 1 qualifies for Discovery Call)
Meeting:Sale Ratio: 2:1 (Each Discovery Call we close 50%)

Conversion Rate:	50% (Cold Traffic)
Conversion Rate:	90% (Referrals)
Sales Cycle:	4-6 weeks (time from lead to contract signed)
Number of Discovery Calls:	88 (Double the number of customers required)
Number of Leads Needed:	264 (3 x the number of discovery calls needed)
Number of Leads Per Week:	5.07 (1 lead a day needed)

We know all these numbers in our business, for every single service. We know how many inbound and outbound leads we need to create to hit our stretch targets as we scale. Your turn. Take one of your products or services and get this all down on paper, using the table below

Total Sales Target (12 months):	
Average Order Value:	
Total New Customers Needed:	
Lead:Meeting Ratio:	
Meeting:Sale Ratio:	
Conversion Rate (Cold Traffic):	
Conversion Rate (Referrals):}	
Length of Sales Cycle:	
Number of Meetings / Calls:	
Number of Leads Needed Total:	
Number of Leads Per Week Needed:	

Do this on repeat for every single product or service. If you need to add in 2nd and 3rd meetings then do that too. The main point here is you need to know your numbers before embarking on any prospecting or outbound activities.

If this was the first time you have gone through this exercise, I hope you found it valuable. if you already know all of this, great. Take it as a solid reminder to track and analyse all of this as it can change depending on your pricing, market conditions, external factors as the last few years have shown us all.

5 ACTIONABLE INSIGHTS FROM THIS CHAPTER

1. Define your pipeline stages with % and implement this in your CRM

2. Work out your sales pipeline numbers using the information provided

3. Repeat for every product or service you sell in your business

4. Look at the actual number of leads coming into your business each week and work out the deficit. How many do you have coming in for each product or service versus what you need to meet your targets.

5. Find a way to track all of this, an Excel sheet or CRM system so that you can get a better handle on your pipeline.

Chapter 2:
Social Selling Index

This chapter and the next couple of chapters are taken from the 2nd edition of 'Linked Inbound' published in July 2022. 'Linked Inbound' came before this one, but the contents of the next few chapters are so important, that I wanted to make sure as a reader that you are either refreshing your knowledge having read my first book, or, if you are hearing about it for the first time, that you have a solid understanding of some of the most fundamental concepts when it comes to social selling success.

There are 3 main overriding principles to focus on when it comesto social selling through LinkedIn®.

- The VCO process
- Understanding your Social Selling Index (SSI)
- The Power of 'Givers Gain'

I am going to explore each of these in detail to get you thinking about how you can apply social selling in your business.

The VCO Process

It is vital that you understand the VCO Process if you are to be successful at marketing your business through LinkedIn®. This process is usually referred to in the world of referral marketing, when networking on a face-to-face basis, and the key is in the power of relationships.

The system of information, support and referrals that you assemble from your networks, bothonline and offline, will be based on your relationships with other individuals and businesses. Referral marketing works because these relationships work both ways and both parties benefit insome way.

The relationship evolves through three phases:

Visibility, Credibility and Opportunity

First you and your business must be visible. Your LinkedIn® profile is your 24/7 digital ambassador, working for you around the clock. This is all about you having a presence online, having a personal profile and a company profile and being seen to be active and engaged on LinkedIn®. Visibility comes from posting great content, having a great profile and being an active member of the LinkedIn® community.

Next, comes credibility, it is not enough just to be visible. Prospects and members of LinkedIn® have got to know, like and trust you before they are going to partwith their money. Always keep in mind that any successful relationship, whether a personal or a business relationship, is unique to every pair of individuals, and it evolves over time. The relationship starts out tentative, fragile, full of unfulfilled possibilities and expectations. It grows stronger with experience and familiarity, and then it matures into trust and commitment.

Credibility online, especially on LinkedIn® is all about how you and your business come across to others, how you start and build relationships, how you position yourself through your profileand in the way you approach relationship building and growing your network.

The VCO Process describes the process of creation, growth and strengthening of business, professional and personal relationships. The main problem with people's lack of understanding of this vital process is that they forget the step that involves the 'C', credibility is all about growing and nurturing the relationship before moving to a sale or moving into a place wheresomeone will refer you to one of their clients.

All too often I see people using LinkedIn® as a selling platform, spamming their network with requests to buy products or services from them, or visit their website. The credibility part is vital if you want to grow your business on LinkedIn®. Rushing into selling destroys your credibility and you may never recover.

"When you sell, you repel!"

Only when you add 'Visibility' to 'Credibility' can you move to Opportunity and profitability in a relationship. When you move the relationship to the next level you will be referred, recommended, promoted and will spread great word of mouth about you and your business. When you are networking online, the VCO Process is even more important as you may not get thechance to actually meet the person you are networking with on a face-to-face basis.

Always bear in mind that:

Visibility + Credibility = Opportunity

This simple concept has made a bigger difference in more people's networking and social selling efforts than any other single idea you will come across and should be remembered as you read this book. Almost every tip in this book is going to relate to either Visibility OR Credibility, and in many cases, both will apply.

Your Social Selling Index (SSI)

What is Social Selling?

According to Wikipedia, Social Selling is the process of developing relationships as part of the sales process. It is about leveraging your social network to find the right prospects, build trusted relationships, and ultimately, achieve your sales goals.

This sales technique enables better sales lead generation and sales prospecting process and eliminates the need for cold calling. Building and maintaining relationships is easier within thenetwork that you and your customer trust.

Prospecting, lead generation and pipeline building via traditional methods are failing. Social selling gives you a competitive edge that gets you seen by your target market.

My core definition of social selling is this:

> "Social selling is the art of selling without selling. It's about building relationships, creating brand awareness, and staying top of mind with both prospects and customers" Sam Rathling

Approximately 95-98% of the people you connect with today are not in the 'buying window' for your products and/or services. Social selling keeps you top of mind, so that when they are ready to buy what you sell, they think of you first.

According to LinkedIn®, social selling leaders create **45%** more opportunities than peers with a lower SSI. Social selling leadersare **51%** more likely to reach quota and **78%** of social sellers outsell peers who don't use social media.

Your Social Selling Index (SSI Score)

Whether you know this, or not, you have a score out of 100 called a Social Selling Index. It is available for free and can help you to benchmark how you are currently performing on LinkedIn®.

The higher your SSI, the higher the chance you will generate leads and real business opportunities. Open LinkedIn® on your desktop or mobile, then open a new tab and go to this link: http://linkedin.com/sales/ssi

You will see an overall score out of 100, this is your SSI as of today, a copy of mine is here for reference. This is updated every24 hours, and once you know how to move the needle on each section you can make dramatic improvements with limited time input. It will look something like this:

Ideally you should be aiming for 75+ as this is where the LinkedIn® magic happens! If you are already over 70 then you are doing an amazing job and there are some small tweaks to bemade. If you are less than 50, don't panic, that is after all the reason you came looking for this book. Within 90 days or so of consistent action we can get you to 75+.

Here is a picture of mine at the time of writing this book:

Your Social Selling Index

Top Industry SSI rank

1%

Top Network SSI rank

1%

Current Social Selling Index ⓘ

87
out of 100

Four components of your score

24.5 | Establish your professional brand ⓘ

19.27 | Find the right people ⓘ

18 | Engage with insights ⓘ

25 | Build relationships ⓘ

People in your industry

26
out of 100

Sales professionals in the Professional Training & Coaching industry have an **average SSI of 26.**

You rank in the **top 1%**

No change since last week

People in your network

49
out of 100

People in your network have an **average SSI of 49.**

You rank in the **top 1%**

No change since last week

How is your Social Selling Index Score Made Up?

There are 4 areas of focus, all equally weighted 25 points. LinkedIn® uses this score to push you towards their premium, paid for services. You can still score over 70 with the free version of LinkedIn®, however to truly elevate your SSI and head into the high 80s and 90s you will need to use Sales Navigator to master the art of social selling in the LinkedIn® environment.

Your SSI score is made up of 4 sections, under the following headings:

Establish your Professional Brand (Orange) – 25 points
Find the Right People (Purple) – 25 points
Engage with Insights (Green) – 25 points
Build Relationships (Blue) – 25 points

SSI - Establish your Professional Brand (Orange Section)

There are 7 main areas within this part of your SSI:

- How Complete your LinkedIn® Profile is
- Multimedia Links in your Profile About section & WorkExperience
- Projects and Publications section completed
- Skills and Endorsement section filled out
- Regular Posts, Articles and Content, Creating followers ofyour Content
- Profile Picture and Banners
- Give Endorsements and Get Endorsements

The more complete your LinkedIn® personal profile, and the moregreat content you post to position yourself as a 'go-to' expert in your field, the higher your orange score will be. This in turn will help you to establish your professional brand.

SSI - Find the Right People (Purple Section)

There are 6 main areas within this part of your SSI Score:

- Use Sales Navigator. For me Sales Navigator is like theFormula 1 Car of LinkedIn®, the problem is that most sales professionals have no idea how to drive it! Having aSales Navigator licence will help to raise your score

- Focus on people searches, using the advanced search feature on Sales Navigator or if you are on the premiumversion, use searches and filters to find people in your target market and add them to your network. This will becovered later.

- Viewing profiles of other people in your target market willhelp your SSI score to go up, you need to be engaged with looking for the right people.

- In addition to you finding other people, you will also scorewhen you generate inbound views to your own profile. The higher the number of profiles you have of the right people, the more your score will increase. You can find this number on the dashboard within your LinkedIn® profile. It's a 90-day statistic.

- Saving leads in Sales Navigator is something you can only do in Navigator. Not only can you find people, you can also save them as leads and follow their activity andposts. They won't know that you have saved them as a lead, but this is a very useful exercise to do on key prospects.

- Daily activity on LinkedIn® or Sales Navigator, will help your score to go higher; being an active user and loggingin daily will increase this score. Consistency is key.

The more prospecting you do, adding the right people into yourLinkedIn® network, the higher the score will be for the purple section of your SSI.

If you are a Sales or Executive Leader and your company has invested in Sales Navigator™ this is a good benchmark to see if your team are actually using it to prospect. Scores less than 12 out of 25 will be a good indication of little or no prospecting activity and is not uncommon. 13-25 and they will most likely be fairly active, however there are so many variables in the success of their prospecting activity as you will learn over the coming chapters.

SSI - Engage with Insights (Green Section)

This is one of the hardest areas to make an impact on, and for many people is often their lowest scoring area. So here are some key pointers on how to increase your 'Engage with Insights' score:

- Engagements given and received: LinkedIn® is looking athow much engagement you are receiving and giving on posts and articles.

- Create content and feed the newsfeed with great posts.

- Share the content of others on your newsfeed.

- Publish articles and engage with people who like,comment and share your content.

- Join LinkedIn® Groups, be an active member in Groups toengage with insights in Groups.

- Regularly save Accounts (Companies) inside of SalesNavigator

- Regularly view Account Pages and scroll the homepageof Companies (Accounts) within LinkedIn® Sales Navigator™

- Use the Alerts and Insights area within Sales Navigator™ including Account Mapping Tools.

SSI - Build Relationships (Blue Section)

The blue section of your LinkedIn® SSI is all about building trusted relationships and is usually the section that scores the highest for most people. Here are some pointers to help you to raise your SSI in the area of relationships:

- Build relationships with Decision Makers
- Engage and start conversations with people whocomment and like your posts
- Prospect regularly, start conversations to build therelationship with people in your target market
- Stay on top of your LinkedIn® inbox and messages, and ifyou have Sales Navigator do the same on your Sales Navigator inbox
- This next one is related to Sales Navigator and InMails only - the messages you send and the % response rate you get from InMails. I am not a huge InMail fan, as it comes across as a sales pitch when you use this feature, but a 10% response or higher can help to move this score

It is usually the easiest part of your SSI to score the highest on.Use this space to write in your SSI score as of today:

My current SSI score is: _____

My target SSI within 90 days is: _____

Note: The lower your starting score, the easier it is to move the needle. A score increase of +10 is achievable within a couple of weeks if you are currently between 30-60 (and follow the advice in this book). If you are already 60-75 it will take more time to move the needle. And if you are over 75 you are already doing well and it will take some slight tweaks to move you into the mid-80's (if you have Sales Navigator™.

5 ACTIONABLE INSIGHTS FROM THIS CHAPTER

1. Check your SSI Score using http://linkedin.com/sales/ssi
2. Take a photo of your score you have a starting point.
3. Record your overall score and your breakdown of each section.
4. Check your Industry ranking (target 1%) and record today's %.
5. Check your Network ranking (target 1%) and record today's %.

Chapter 3: IDEAL Client & Pains

Knowing your Target Market

Before tackling any kind of social selling, especially on LinkedIn®, you need to truly understand your target market. Most companies can and do serve a wide range of industry sectors and different types of clients.

There are some key considerations to look at when you considering what your focus is going to be within the LinkedIn® environment. Some companies call this their customer avatar or customer personas and have a really detailed description of this information, others have never really stopped to think about it!

So what type of things can you consider when you are thinking about your IDEAL client?

You may have 2 or 3 target markets. At Pipeline 44 we have a range of products and services that suit a micro-business; then we have products and services that suit mid-size clients scaleups, finally we have solutions for multinational, enterprise corporate clients. We have done this exercise for each target market and have a clear picture of what eachone looks like.

From this we have been able to create a Top 100 list for target key accounts. We are very clear about who we want to do business with, and all of our social selling and marketing efforts are based on knowing these target markets inside out. This then feeds our LinkedIn® profiles, our content delivery and our marketing efforts throughout the entire sales process.

To help, I have created a model called the IDEAL client template to help you and your teams with this. When you complete this exercise for each target market, write out a description of your ideal client. Not the clients you have at the moment, the ones you really want in the future. When I say IDEAL, I mean the ones who will bring you the highest revenue, profit and/or commission.

Take some time to think about this and write this down using the table I have provided. The success of every strategy I am going to give you in this book hinges on you knowing, really knowing, and understanding your target market.

I.D.E.A.L Client Framework

This IDEAL client framework can help you narrow your focus andthink about these 5 core areas for your IDEAL client:

I   **Industries:** Verticals, Sectors, Types of Business

D **Demographic**: Size, Years Established, Staff, Revenue, Type of Company

E **Experience:** Job Titles of Key Targets, Background, Role & Responsibility

A **Attributes:** Values, Ambitions, Culture, What Do they Have in Common?

L **Location:** Geography, Towns, Cities, Regions, where do you want them?

Here is an example from my own business, this is for what we call in our business 'Tier 3'. These are companies which are scaling up, usually investor or VC backed, with sales teams in significant growth. They are not the market leader yet but are chomping at the bit to scale and grow, to take market share fast.

IDEAL Client	Description
Industries	Software; SaaS; Hardware; Tech; Fintech; EdTech; Blockchain; AI; Consulting; Information Technology.
Demographic	Sales team of 25+; Revenue over £50m; 5-10 years in business; investor or VC backed, scaling up fast.
Experience	Chief Revenue Officer, Chief Sales Officer, Head of Sales Enablement, EMEA Sales Director, VP of Sales, European Sales Director, Commercial Director.
Attributes	Hires top sales talent; People Focused; Ambitious Growth Plans, Founders on path to exit within 5 years.
Location	Globally, ideally English speaking countries across EMEA, APAC, US.

I recommend spending some time on this. If you believe you can serve everyone and anyone and you are finding this task hard, then look back over your last 10 clients. Create a spreadsheet and write down the IDEAL acronym of each one.

Look for the commonality, look for the similarities in industry sector, size of company etc. You'll start to recognise patterns.

To help you, I have provided a template for you to complete your own here:

http://pipeline44.com/ideal-pains

P.A.I.N.S Framework

Now that you know more about what your IDEAL client looks like, it's important that you also think about the solutions that you provide for them. This starts by you truly understanding their pain points, challenges, and problems.

Let's take a look at some questions that will start you thinking about this:

- What problems do you solve?

- Why do clients come to you?

- What frustrations do they have?

- What challenges cause them to need your products and/or services?

- What kind of payoff do they want?

- What do they want to improve?

- What do they want to gain?

Every day you hear about pain points from your clients. They should come up in every phone call and every meeting that you undertake with a potential client during the discovery phase. You can use this framework as a guide.

PAINS Framework for your IDEAL client

To help you, I have developed a PAINS profile template for you to complete, when you do so, have your IDEAL client template at the forefront of your mind.

P   **Problems:** What problems do you solve for your clients?

A   **Agony:** What keeps them awake at night?

I   **Issues:** What are some of the symptoms and issues?

N   **Nagging:** What annoys or frustrates them?

S   **Struggles:** What do they struggle with?

Having a deep understanding of the problems you solve for your clients is critical to your success. It will help you:

- Develop great content that actually gets you inbound leads.

- Write a powerful profile that turns profile viewers into inquiries

- Construct outreach messages that actually get a response

Spend time on this part of my book, I don't recommend skimming over it or ignoring it. You can download the IDEAL and PAINS template here:

https://pipeline44.com/ideal-pains

What I have learnt over my 22 years of sales experience, is that the REAL problem is never the problem that the prospect brings you. There is always an underlying, emotion fuelled reason for the conversation they are having with you.

This is another tool that will help you. It's an emotions wheel. When you go through the PAINS, think about combining them with some of these words. What emotions are your clients feeling?

Emotions Wheel

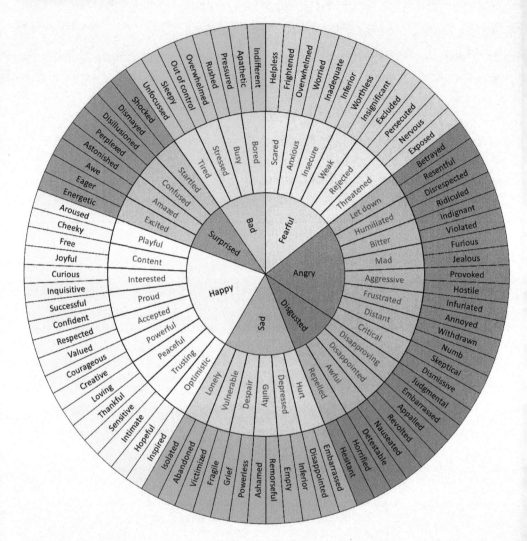

Once you have a clear picture of your target market and a strongly developed IDEAL and PAINS framework, everything on becomes SO much easier! When I work with sales teams and business owners, this is one of the first things I focus on with my delegates. Why? Because it is so fundamental to social selling success!

As with the IDEAL framework, I have written out an example of PAINS for my Tier 3 target markets, so you can use this as an example.

PAINS Framework	Description
Problems	Not enough sales opportunities in the pipeline; not enough qualified leads; heavily invested in Sales Navigator™ and not seeing a return on their investment; salespeople spending hours on LinkedIn® but getting minimal results; sales team prospecting efforts and getting less than 3% response rate; can't get the team to share content; they just don't 'get' the importance of social selling for building their sales pipeline.
Agony	Sales Director, CRO or CSO is worried about hitting targets, concerned about losing their job or securing their promotion if they can't get a handle on their sales pipeline. Missing targets, under pressure, lacking commission, causing problems at home. Working longer hours, stressed out.
Issues	Not enough quality or quantity of leads in the pipeline. The leads they do have are not quality. No inbound leads at all, it all seems like a big effort. Attrition in the team, people are leaving.
Nagging	Marketing are not providing enough qualified leads, sales team are complaining about a lack of leads. Conflict in the team, some leaving, some not pulling their weight. Morale is low in the team. CRM never up to date.
Struggles	Struggling to get their team to get business from LinkedIn®, they are either a 'can't do' or a 'won't do'. Most are very traditional and set in their ways, trying to get them to do anything on social is a struggle.

5 ACTIONABLE INSIGHTS FROM THIS CHAPTER

1. Download the IDEAL / PAINS template (or create your own).

2. Create an IDEAL client for each target market you serve.

3. If you aren't sure look back over your last 10 clients and look for commonality.

4. Create a PAINS profile for each target market that you serve.

5. Use the emotions wheel to add depth to your PAINS framework.

Chapter 4:
Positioning and Profile

Before we get into the complexities of prospecting and outreach on LinkedIn®, it's important to take a moment to consider your positioning for this platform as well are how you are presenting yourself to potential prospects, through your LinkedIn® profile.

Your profile is your digital ambassador for both you and your team. It's networking for you 24/7, 365 days a year, it's out there promoting you and your business when you are asleep, when you are on holiday and when you are in meetings. It's networking for you whilst you are reading my book.

An outbound approach will most definitely drive up your profile views. People will check out your LinkedIn profile before deciding to connect with you. If your profile has the right keywords to get you found, you will drive up profile views.

Many people don't realise that your profile is like a mini-web page with its own SEO and keywords, that don't just get you found on LinkedIn®, they also get you found on Google too. At the time of writing this, I rank on Page 1 of Google organically for the search term 'LinkedIn expert'. It's not my website that shows up, it's my LinkedIn profile, and there are literally hundreds of thousands of results that come up, yet mine is up there for free, I don't pay Google a penny to rank on Page 1.

Does it get me business? Absolutely. Could yours be ranking on Page 1, absolutely. There are seven places in your LinkedIn® personal profile where you can sneak in keywords, without making it look like you've done so.

The way you position yourself, bearing in mind the previous chapters on IDEAL and PAINS, is key to you getting responses from potential prospects. A lot of this book is designed to help Sales Leaders and their teams but can also be applied if you are in a leadership role, marketing function or running your own business.

I run training sessions with salespeople in corporate and enterprise accounts, who come to me saying they aren't getting business from LinkedIn®. As part of my pre-training audit, it's not surprising, especially when I visit their LinkedIn® profiles and read their professional headlines which include words like "Business Development Manager at…", "Sales Executive at…", "Account Manager at…".

They not only look like a salesperson, but they are also acting like one too. In many cases their profiles read like bad online CV's, the profile is all about them, their skills, their experience and doesn't mention their customers, the business they represent and how they help their clients. They wonder why they are getting little or no response from their outreach or InMails™, well it all starts with their profile and positioning.

If the sales team set themselves up to look professional, customer focused, seen as trusted advisors, with a complete focus on their IDEAL client and how they help solve their PAINS, they would have way more success. It's the same for business owners too, their outreach is not working and lot of that has to do with how they are positioning themselves on their LinkedIn® profile.

TASK: Go look at your profile and if relevant, the profile of each of your teams.

Now ask yourself these questions:

> "Would you become a customer of you (or your team member) today, based on what the LinkedIn® profile says?"
>
> "Would you reply to message if this person prospected you?"
>
> "Would you send a message on LinkedIn® wanting to meet this person because of how clear it is that they can help you?"

In most cases the answers to the above questions are 'no'. Before outbound can be effective this needs to be addressed. You will significantly increase the amount of prospects who accept your invitation to connect by spending time first on your profile and positioning. This makes prospecting more efficient and will increase acceptance rates.

Imagine that your IDEAL client is reading your profile right now. They are in the market for what you sell, and they have pain or problem you can fix. They come across your profile.

What do they need to see, read, and hear for them to be compelled to take action? Does your profile give enough call to action? Your profile should be customer-centric, aimed completely at your IDEAL client. It should help the person visiting your profile to take the next step, whether that's to learn more, research you (without leaving your profile), or to contact you.

There are, at the time of writing this book, there are 20 different areas of your LinkedIn® profile to pay attention to. Some will be obvious, and others are features that have only recently been introduced by LinkedIn® and they may be completely new to you.

The 20 Elements of your LinkedIn profile

1. Header Image (1584 x 396 pixels)

2. Professional Headshot / Photograph
3. Profile Video (30 Second Video Intro)

4. Your Name

5. Name Pronunciation (10 Second Audio)

6. Pronouns (he/him; she/her; them/they etc.)

7. Professional Headline (220 Characters)

8. Contact Information

9. Lead Magnet or Web Link

10. About Section (2600 Characters)

11. Featured Section (Media, Links, Documents, Posts, Articles)

12. Work Experience

13. Projects & Publications

14. Voluntary Experience

15. Skills & Endorsements

16. Recommendations

17. Honours and Awards

18. Keywords to get you found

19. Creator Mode (Choose on or off)

20. All Star Profile

I go into a lot of detail about setting up an effective LinkedIn profile in my accompanying book 'Linked Inbound' as well as on my podcast 'Social Selling with Sam' so I am not going to go into lots of detail in this book as there are plenty of other resources to help you with this.

My main focus for this chapter is to make you aware that you have some work to do, before you start prospecting. Paying attention to this now, will pay dividends in the long run. Spend some time updating it and checking your profile before you launch into and outbound prospecting campaign.

One area I do want to help you with, especially those in sales function, is your professional headline. This is the 220 characters that sits below your name and is the first thing that a prospect sees.

If you have 'Job Title at Company X' as the main headline under your name, you are going to instantly put off a potential prospect when you try to outreach to them. If your job title has 'sales', 'business development', 'account management' or anything related to selling you are going to get less acceptances from decision makers. Aim to make your 220 characters all about your clients, how you solve their problems, how you help. You can include your actual job title in your Work Experience section and/or your About section.

Whenever a client comes to us for help with their social selling campaigns, the first step is always undertaking a LinkedIn® makeover, so that we can make their profile match their IDEAL and PAINS and focus on the right things for the purpose of their content and/or prospecting campaign. The same applies when clients book me to work with their teams, there is always a foundational piece of work we need to undertake on the team company profiles, before we launch into training on prospecting, engagement, and content.

So now it's time for some actions to help you sort out your profile ahead of any outbound activity.

5 ACTIONABLE INSIGHTS FROM THIS CHAPTER

1. Update your LinkedIn profile About Section to match your IDEAL and PAINS.

2. Check your contact information is up to date.

3. Record a 30 second profile video (in the LinkedIn® mobile app).

4. Go through the list of 20 elements and complete any sections you don't have.

5. Update your Featured section with media relevant to your IDEAL client.

Chapter 5:
8 Different Ways to Prospect

Prospecting is getting harder. Fact.

LinkedIn reported in Q3 2021 that they have seen a 40% drop in response rates to InMails (not that I am a fan of using them at all – more on that later).

The average number of prospecting messages being received by decision-makers on average is 10 per day, that's 50 a week, 200 a month! So how do you cut through the noise? How do you stand out from the crowd and drive a response rate that makes it worth all the effort?

Having spent over a decade mastering the art of prospecting on LinkedIn, I have refined this into 8 different ways you can prospect on LinkedIn, depending on the outcome you want and more your style and tone of voice. Four of these are more likely to end up in sales leads, and the other four are more likely to build your pipeline for the future.

- Network Building Only
- Prospecting for Talent

- Relationship Building
- Filling Your Events
- Starting Sales Conversations
- Added Value Give Away
- Key Account Targeting
- Brand Building Only

Before I go into detail on each one, it is important to note that the success of your prospecting efforts is not solely reliant on your outreach message, frequency or consistency. There are many factors that make a prospecting campaign effective, including having a profile that matches the ideal client you are targeting, posting content that really speaks to your ideal client as well as regular engagement on the newsfeed.

To make it even more effective, combining a prospecting campaign with more traditional methods is also important. Picking up the phone to new connections and people who did not respond to your prospecting outreach, massively increases the number of meetings and opportunities in your pipeline, but so few people do this.

Another important note, is to avoid shortcuts, don't be tempted by automation tools, you risk getting your LinkedIn account banned and you are likely to damage your reputation by sending out automated messages and sequences that are clearly driven by AI. The more you can personalise your connection requests, the higher your response rate will be (our Sales Manager has an acceptance rate of over 70%). We use 3 out of 20 possible personalisation points when connecting with our target market, always making sure we spend time viewing the person's profile first, before connecting.

So now that I have established some fundamentals, let's get into the detail of each type of prospecting campaign.

1. Network Building Only

This is the simplest of ways to prospect, simply adding connections of those people who fit your ideal client profile. You can simply add 5-20 people a day into your network who are an exact match to the type of people you want to be connected with.

Once connected you can build your brand, they may see your content and they may engage once you have built up your visibility and credibility with them. With this type of prospecting campaign, there is no follow-up sequence, simply adding new connections into your network. I use this approach with influencers, and people in very senior roles that I am not ready to prospect yet. So right now my personal prospecting focus is on companies with £5m-500m turnover with sales teams, usually scale-up technology companies for example.

I want to be connected to CMO's, CEO's and CCO's in multi-billion turnover businesses, Right now, I simply want them in my network, so that when I am ready to go to market with transformational change programmes, they will already have spent a year getting to understand me and what my company is about through my content, articles, and posts. In a few months from now, we will retarget them with a prospecting message designed to land meetings, but only when we are ready to do so.

Connection to Invite: 40-60%

2. Prospecting for Talent: Build the Bench

The fight for talent is unbelievable right now. Having spent 14 years in recruitment I understand how to find, attract, and reach out to passive candidates who are not currently looking for a role. When the market is so candidate-driven, it is critical that companies understand how to prospect for talent, and this should be happening ALL the time, not just when a vacancy arises.

Prospecting for talent is about building the bench, it's about having conversations with talented people in your industry and beyond who may or may not be looking for a move, and building relationships now so that when you do have a position available you can proactively recruit and have 5-10 x A-players ready take to the next stage who have already confirmed that they like what they see, already have an interest in your brand and want to interview as soon as a role becomes available.

If you have high attrition or are growing rapidly and you don't have a prospecting campaign running for your core roles, you are missing an opportunity, plus the costs that can be saved here are huge, especially if your traditional route is agencies and advertising.

Connection to Invite: 40-60%. **Invite to positive response:** 15%.

3. Relationship Building

We've all had them, the sleazy sales pitch that lands in your inbox and doesn't make any attempt to build a relationship first.
It's all about them, their company, their amazing life-changing widget or service. Yuck!

Well, this type of prospecting campaign will suit those who aren't really in sales or consider themselves not very 'salesy' in their approach. For you, it's all about the relationship. This type of prospecting will result in less real tangible leads, but more conversations with the right types of people. The outreach message here should still all be about the other person, but ask a question that leads to a conversation and an opportunity for you to build the relationship.

If you are in sales or run a sales team, especially if you are more into consultative selling then this one could work for you, but if you have sales targets to meet and want to book meetings now, I wouldn't go with this one. This is a long term play and is likely to lead to lots of conversations and new relationships but fewer sales meetings.

Connection to Invite: 40-60%. **Expected response rate:** 5%.

4. Filling Your Events

I love this one, as it is the highest converting type of sales-focused campaign when the event topic is strong, and the content delivered at the event is good. Our most successful campaigns for clients involve events and it is what drives our own lead-gen machine.

Whether you are running live in-person events and workshops, or whether you are running online events such as webinars, LinkedIn is a great way to fill these events, both from prospecting and from the LinkedIn events feature. You can use the messaging and outreach to gain interest in your event and get more delegates registered.

Now, they aren't all going to show up, and that's OK, but typically at the moment we are seeing a 70% show rate to our free online events and from that, we are booking meetings, and then moving people to either in-person 2-Day Masterclasses, my Pipeline Academy which is my online course and group mentoring, and some go on to speak to us about outsourced solutions.
If you are running online or offline events to feed your business with leads, and you are not using LinkedIn to fill your events, you are missing a trick. This is one of the best ways to fill your sales pipeline.

Connection to Invite: 50%. Expected response rate: 15%.

5. Starting Sales Conversations

My favourite, as it is the one that delivers the most revenue. It's not everyone's cup of tea, but this is a very effective type of prospecting campaign.

When used with decision-makers who have the exact pain points that you can fix, the 'PAINKILLER' formula that I teach our clients, is a winner. It involves making the follow-up message focused on the pain points of that specific job title and asking a killer question designed to start a sales conversation.

Prospecting using sales conversations always results in meetings and at the very least a prospect who is surprised and delighted by the approach, which is completely different to the usual sales pitches landing in their inbox. This format is tried and tested and has secured the most amount of business for our own companies and for our clients.

WARNING: If you are not good at selling or don't consider yourself to be a salesperson, then avoid this type of campaign! You have to be able to ask great questions and move the conversation offline for this one to be effective.

Connection to Invite: 50%.

Expected response rate: 3-5% **When using video:** 30-40%

6. Added Value - Give Away

If you have something that is of major interest to prospects, or very high perceived value, then the giveaway campaign could be good for your business. It can't be boring like a white paper, but something that the prospect would regard as useful to them or helpful.

It could be an invitation to take part in a round table, with peers which they would normally have to pay for, it could be a free copy of a book, it could be industry research that is not publicly available and would be very insightful to your potential prospect. Ideally, this should not involve any opt-in and it should not be gated content. So in other words, not a link to a page where they have to enter their email address to get it. That won't work.

This type of campaign can provide you with solid leads, from people who have a genuine interest in what you have to offer and will see you as being useful, trusted and helpful to them by providing it.

Connection to Invite: 50%. **Expected response rate:** 5-7%

7. Added Value Give Away

If you or your sales team are focused on a select number of key accounts, a target hit list of potential clients, then this type of prospecting campaign is designed to secure a footprint across with depth and breadth of the organisation. In this approach, you would want to connect with the full cast of characters that could be involved in the decision-making process. From the economic buyers, who are signing off the budget, to technical buyers and user buyers.

When we help clients run these types of campaigns, we usually focus on 6-7 job titles within one organisation, with the aim of securing at least half of them as new connections. Sales Navigator makes it easy to build an Account Map and then from there we can look at other people in the organisation who may be useful to target.

Sales cycles are typically 18-24 months with these campaigns, so it is also important to nurture, engage and post so that the people in these target accounts also keep your brand top of mind. A Key Account campaign should include a follow-up message, designed to start the conversation, however, it is important to bear in mind that the buying window for most of these prospects will be small, especially if what you sell has 3-5 year contracts and there is an incumbent supplier in place that you are looking to replace.

Connection to Invite: 50%. **Invite to positive response:** 3-5%.

8. Brand Building Only

If you already have a significant network, and you don't need hundreds of leads per month, you may decide to focus on brand building only. This is where your lead activity comes inbound because of your thought leadership, personal brand, influence and content.

Done well this can drive significant inbound leads, but most salespeople and business owners don't have the network or audience following to make this happen straight away. A Brand Building campaign should consist of posting at least 3-5 times per week either on your own or with the support of a content marketing agency. Content, when it is engaging, emotive and relatable, will secure thousands of views and drive inbound enquiries. But for most this does not happen.

I have spent a decade building my personal brand, building my following, increasing my positioning and influence in my space and I generate inbound leads on a daily basis. I also know many other clients who generate enough inbound leads to secure them a steady pipeline of leads, but for most, you would need to combine brand building with one of the above 7 types of campaigns. It is not enough to only post content, you also need to prospect at the same time, so the right people see your content and get to know, like and trust you.

Inbound Leads per month: 3-12 depending on size of network and your influence level.

Decide which is the most relevant for your business, you may decide to use a combination. We use sales conversations, events and network building as a team, and we run 5 campaigns across 5 separate profiles in our business. If you aren't prospecting at all, then start. Just start.

If you aren't prospecting, you aren't filling your pipeline and that will impact your bottom line.

5 ACTIONABLE INSIGHTS FROM THIS CHAPTER

1. Decide on which style(s) of prospecting you feel would suit your business

2. Set your targets for acceptance rates (invite:connection)

3. Set your targets for response rates (connection:response)

4. Decide how you will track and measure your activity (a spreadsheet or CRM)

5. Set your target number of new connections and by when as well as your target number of leads/revenue from your prospecting efforts (bear in mind it will take you 90-120 days of consistency to have enough data to benchmark and start gaining traction).

NOTE: Remember social selling is a marathon, not a sprint.

Chapter 6: Outreach Messages, Building Connections

Outreach can be a scary thing to a lot of people. Many people I speak to worry about coming across too 'salesy' or 'cringy' as there are so many salespeople and business owners getting their outreach wrong. I personally receive on average 5-10 bad sales approaches per day into my LinkedIn® inbox, which I love as my sales team turn every one into a lead for our agency. However, if you know that 5-10 per day is the average for decision makers across the platform, you will recognise that getting your outreach right is key to your success.

When I was a kid, my Dad was a Bank Manager, a very good one. He regularly moved branches with each promotion he was given and this meant that every 18-24 months we had to move house as a family. With that, a new school for me and my sisters and every time we moved location. At the time I didn't like it at all, I'd make new friends and then I'd have to move again, and repeat this. I attended 6 different schools by the age of sixteen.

I've been turning strangers into friends since I was 5 years old. Now I see that those skills I gained from a young age were simply turning me into a master networker. I am very good at building connections, turning a cold contact into a strong professional relationship. I've always been good at networking face to face, in-person, and now I am also great at doing this online, on platforms like LinkedIn®. So now I look back on my early years as a solid education that has led me to what I do now.

This is the simplest way I can put outreach on LinkedIn®. It's about building relationships, by turning strangers into friends.

There are many ways you can approach prospecting; you have already seen in the last chapter that there are 8 different prospecting campaign types. This chapter looks at how you can secure acceptances from the people you approach as well as how to follow up once you have secured a new connection.

I like to keep things simple, so I recommend a simple two-step approach to starting a conversation. Don't think I need to get a meeting, or I need to book a call. Think I need to build a relationship and start a conversation that may turn into a lead. We'll talk about the different types of leads to expect in Chapter 9 (more on that later).

So this chapter will be in two parts:

Message 1 – To Secure the Connection
Message 2 – To Start the Conversation

Message 1 – Secure the Connection

In May 2021, LinkedIn® introduced a new limitation on all of it's members (including paying clients), restricting outreach to a maximum of 100 invites per week. This was in response to complaints from members and the high number of automation tools on the market which were, and still are, being used to short cut the process, with members using A.I bots to prospect for them. This is NOT recommended! You risk losing your LinkedIn® account forever, LinkedIn® is really clamping down on automation, to stop the spamming and the high numbers of connection requests being sent out by these tools. I am not a fan and you can ALWAYS tell when someone is using automation. It's horrible and I really don't recommend it in your outreach.

With only 100 invitations a week, you need to ensure that you are securing a minimum of 40% acceptance rate when you reach out to potential prospects in your IDEAL target market. If you are getting way less than this right now, there will be something in your outreach message that is not working. Hopefully this chapter will help.

If you are a Sales Navigator™ or Premium LinkedIn user, ie. You are paying for LinkedIn solutions, you will have access to a certain number of InMails™ per month, which is a product that LinkedIn® heavily promotes in the sales process, and offers to paying clients. I am NOT a fan of InMails™. To me they scream that you are trying to sell someone something, and they can be deleted easily and ignored. When someone deletes your InMail™ or chooses to ignore it, they are not choosing to be a part of your network, let alone respond to you! By them choosing not to be in your network, they don't even become a connection, and will never see any content you post in the future.

At least if someone accepts you into their network, you stand a chance later on of turning them into a prospect or client, because that's when the relationship starts. They may not respond to your outreach, but at least you have the chance to build your visibility and credibility with them over time. We regularly receive inbound leads from people that initially ignored our outreach, but months later after seeing our content and consistent value-adding in the newsfeed, they come back when the are in the buying window, and are looking for some help. If they had rejected an InMail™ that would never have happened. So if you are using InMails for prospecting, choose if you want to continue down that path.

I do use InMail™ sometimes as securing a 10% or higher response rate does have a positive impact on my SSI score, so I typically will use them with people I know, or have recently met as they are likely to accept me, which is a big tick in the algorithm for LinkedIn's SSI reporting.

So if you are not using InMail™ or don't have Sales Navigator™ (yet) then you will simply be using the 'Connect' method, where you can add the person and 'Add a note' when you reach out. This is the most effective method for securing a high acceptance rate, and this acceptance rate will be significantly increased, the more you put effort into your outreach.

There are a number of ways to increase acceptance rates:

- Hyper-personalisation
- Follow and engage first
- Connecting with your followers

We will look at each one in more detail in this chapter to help you. My Sales Manager secures a 74% acceptance rate on her connection messages, and she uses all of these methods to ensure that when she is prospecting that as many of her IDEAL client as possible accept her into their network, and go on to see her amazing content about social selling, sales and prospecting.

Hyper-Personalised Prospecting

Personalisation is all about building rapport, demonstrating to your potential new connection that you have taken the time to properly look at their profile, that you are not using any form of automation and that you care about attention to detail. It is important that they don't feel you are just sending the same old generic 'copy and paste' message to every person that looks like them.

The aim of hyper-personalisation is to:

"Show me that you know me"

When done well, and if your profile looks the part as well as your targeting being relevant, you should be able to secure an acceptance rate of 50% of higher. I have come up with a list of 20 personalisation points that you can use to personalise your connection requests.

20 Personalisation Points

1. Mutual Connections

We already reference this in your 1st messages (2nd degree only), but will be more specific:

If less than 10:   "I see we have some mutual connections."

If 11-50:   "I see we have over 30 mutual connections (go up in 10's)"

If over 50:   "I notice that we share so many mutual connections, I cannot believe we haven't come across each other before now!"

2. Shared University

If not at same time: "I also saw that we both went to (Name of University)."

If at the same time: "By coincidence, I see that we both went to (Name of University) and were there at the same time!"

3. Shared Education Topic

"I saw that we both studied a similar subject, (Insert Subject)"

"I saw that we both studied (Insert Subject)"

"I saw that we both have a degree in (Insert Subject"

4. Shared LinkedIn Groups

"I see that we are both members of the 'Sales Enablement Thought Leadership Exchange' LinkedIn group."

5. Volunteer Work / Charity Work

"I saw that you also do (volunteer /community) work."

"I see that you are also a Trustee for a Charity. I love the work I do for (Insert Charity)"

6. Length of Time in Role or at Company

"I noticed that you have been with (Company Name) for over 5 years"

"It's impressive that you've been with (Company Name) for more than 9 years."

"I see you've been (Insert Job Title) for more than XX years."

7. Followers (only use for 5k Followers or more):

"I see you've built up an impressive following of over (Insert Followers) here on LinkedIn."

"I was impressed that you have over XXXX Followers"

8. Something Impressive (Stroke the Ego)

"I was impressed with (Insert Impressive Thing) on your profile."

"Congratulations on your MBE status."

"I was impressed that you are a Fellow of (Insert Name of Industry Body)."

"Love your Featured Section of your profile. The videos are great"

9. Strong Content – Articles & Posts

"I've been impressed with your recent posts"

"I have been following your content and I'm impressed with your most recent Article"

"I've seen how much of an effort you've been making on building your brand"

Note: It helps if you've recently liked or commented on their post(s).
Only use if they are posting original content and writing Articles (recently).

10. Recommendations

If 20+:   "I was impressed with your high number of LinkedIn recommendations."
If Less: "I was reading through some of your impressive recommendations."

11. Uniqueness or Different – A Stand Out Something

Often, we will come across a profile that stands out in some way, it could be their banner, their professional headline, their mission, their LinkedIn headshot. If we see it, we'll say it:

"Wow! What a great header image"
"I absolutely love your profile picture, it's really different!"
"Your headline really caught my attention. It's really unique."

12. Quirky Company Name or Branding

"I couldn't help but notice your quirky company name. How did you come up with it?"
"What an interesting company name!"
"Love your branding, it's fantastic!"

13. Hobbies & Interests

"I couldn't help but notice on your profile that we share a passion for (Insert Hobby or Interest)"
"I am also a huge (Insert Hobby or Interest) fan. I've been playing for XX years.
"I saw on your profile that you are into (Insert Hobby or Interest)".

14. Publications

Not everyone uses this section of their profile, if they do then there will usually be things you can reference:

"I saw that you were recently featured in (Insert Publication Name)."
"Congratulations on being a published Author."
"I saw that you have an impressive number of publications"

15. Awards & Achievements

"I was really impressed with all of your Awards and Achievements."

"I saw that you were recently awarded (insert award)"

"Well done on all of your Awards and Achievements, I saw that you were awarded (insert Award name"

16. Languages they Speak

"I saw that you speak a few different languages. Impressive."

"I noticed you have a few different languages listed on your profile."

17. Change of Circumstance (New Role Same Company / New Job)

You can use Sales Navigator to find people in new jobs in the last 90 Days:

"I noticed that you've recently changed jobs"

"I saw that you've only been in your role for a few months."

"How's the new role going for you? I saw you've recently made a move/been promoted"

18. Milestone (Work Anniversary / Birthday)

You may happen to notice this when prospecting

"Congratulations! I noticed it's your work anniversary today / this week."

"Congratulations! Happy Birthday! I hope you're having a lovely day."

19. Same Home Town / Grew Up in Same Place

You can sometimes glean this from their Education Section, Primary & Secondary schools if listed are good places to find this information.

"I couldn't help but notice that you are from the same home town as me!"

"I also grew up in (Insert Town Name)"

"What a coincidence, I saw that we share the same home town!"

20. Industry Match

"I see we've both been in the (Insert Industry Type) for a long time."

"I couldn't help but notice that we've been in the same industry as each other for some time"

"I can't believe our paths haven't crossed! We've both been in (Industry) for a long time."

1st Message Templates for Personalisation

You only have 300 characters in the 'Add a note' section on connection requests, if you choose to use InMail™ you are not restricted in the same way. Below are some suggested messages you could use to get someone to connect with you. Use your own style and voice and adapt as you see necessary. These are only guidance. All of this does take a lot of time, but is worth it for you to increase your network and gain acceptance from enough people in your IDEAL client target market to make a difference to you sales pipeline.

Less than 10 mutual connections:

Hi (First Name),

I saw that (Personalisation Point 1), and that we (Personalisation Point 2). When I looked at your profile I also noticed that we have some mutual connections."

Let's Connect

(Your Name)

11-50 Mutual Connections:

Hi (First Name),

I saw that (Personalisation Point 1), and that we (Personalisation Point 2). When I looked at your profile I also noticed that we have over XX shared connections."

Let's connect

(Your Name)

More than 50 Mutual Connections:

Hi (First Name),

I saw that (Personalisation Point 1), and that we (Personalisation Point 2). When I looked at your profile I also noticed that share so many mutual connections, I cannot believe we haven't come across each other before now!"

Shall we connect?

(Your Name)

Connection Volumes

As I already mentioned, you are limited to 100 invites per week. I do recommend sending 1st messages, connection requests daily. If you have a healthy sales pipeline and you are a business owner juggling lots of hats, managing clients as well as sales, then aim to get at least 5 a day sent.

If you are in a pure business development role, then I would expect as an absolute minimum that you would be sending 10 invitations per day out, that's 50 a week, 200 a month. If you really want to smash your sales quota and fill your sales pipeline and acquire key logos for your company, then 20 a day.

At Pipeline 44, we send 20 messages per day in our IDEAL, usually first thing every day so that it gets done. We then follow them all up with a 2nd message (more on that shortly), then our sales team spends the rest of the day cold calling the people we have recently invited to connect, or having meetings with the people who have responded positively. At the time of writing this we book 6-12 meetings a week with C-Suite decision makers in our IDEAL client target market for Corporates and Scale Ups.

What are your sales team achieving from their LinkedIn prospecting efforts?

If they are not prospecting daily, they are losing you money. If they are not picking up the phone to their new connections, they are losing you money. If they are not starting conversations daily with your IDEAL client, they are leaving money on the table. This can all be done in less than 1 hour a day, so there really is no excuse!

Follow First & Engage Approach

Hitting the 'Follow' button first, on the profile of someone you are going to connect with can be a good way to get on their radar and increase acceptance rates. That person will be notified you are now following their content, and they

43

may start showing up in your LinkedIn newsfeed. You wouldn't do this for every person, but you could sporadically do this to increase acceptance. This will also help with your SSI score as LinkedIn® will see this as additional engagement with your network.

Connecting with Followers

If you choose to put your profile into Creator Mode, you will change your profile to 'Follow' only, the option to 'Connect' with you will disappear, don't worry it's still there, just in a hidden menu. Those followers may start seeing your content on their newsfeed. You will pick up new followers but not all of these new followers will connect with you. Some just choose to follow your content. Once in a while, go through your recent Followers and personalise the request.

Use this link to see your Followers: https://www.linkedin.com/feed/followers/

Here is a suggestion of a message you could use to connect with recent followers:

"Hi (First Name),

I noticed that you've recently started following my content here on LinkedIn. Just wanted to drop you a quick note to say thank you, I really appreciate it.

I look forward to being connected with you.

(Your Name)

I like this one, as I can pick and choose who I am adding into my network. I am getting pickier now as I am fast approaching the 30,000 connections limit, you can have unlimited followers but you max out at 30,000 connections.

Connecting with Profile Viewers

Another source of new connections, where acceptance rates will be higher is your recent profile viewers You can see these in your dashboard on your LinkedIn profile. Profile views is anyone who has visited your profile in the last 90 days. If you have a free LinkedIn® account, then you will only see the previous 5 visitors. On a Sales Navigator™ licence or a Premium licence, you will see all profile viewers.

Each week, go through your recent profile views who are still showing as 2nd or 3rd degree connections and have a job title that is useful to you (think back again to your IDEAL client). This means that they will have visited your profile but are still not connected with you. Personalise the request to thank them for visiting and ask them to connect. Here is an example message that I use that secures me around 80% acceptance rate:

"Hi (First Name),

Thanks for viewing my LinkedIn profile. After viewing yours, it would be great to have you in my network to learn from and network with you.

I look forward to being connected.

(Your Name)"

Be sure to make a visit to their profile if you are going to use this template.

All of the methods mentioned so far in this chapter will significantly increase your acceptance rate, and help you to build your network with the right people.

Message 2 – Start the Conversation

The second message you use to start a conversation will largely depend on the type of campaign you want to run, based on the previous chapter. These are all very outcome based, here I will provide various examples that you can use and adapt to your own business.

These are examples only, you should spend time developing your 2nd messages to start the conversation and you will need lots of different versions for the different buyers and IDEAL clients you are going after. Every job function will have different pain points and therefore this is not a one size fits all solution.

1. An example to start Sales Conversations: PAIN Killer

Many thanks for accepting my connection request (First Name).

In my conversations with (Job Titles), I'm hearing (EMOTION 1) with (PAIN 1), some are (EMOTION 2) with (PAIN 2) and others are (EMOTION 3) with (PAIN 3).

(Insert Killer Question)

Kind regards

(First Name)

I describe this as a PAIN killer formula: Pain + Pain + Pain + Killer Question.

Killer Question Examples:

On a scale of 1-10, how confident are you…. (10 = Highly Confident)

On a scale of 1-10, how would you rate… (10 = Exceptional)

How are you finding… (insert topic)

What has been your experience of…

When you are (insert emotion), how do you…

If you could wave a magic wand, what one thing would you change about…

2. An Example to Invite People to an Event:

Many thanks for connecting with me (First Name).

In my conversations with (Job Titles), I'm hearing (EMOTION 1) with (PAIN 1), some are (EMOTION 2) with (PAIN 2) and others are (EMOTION 3) with (PAIN 3).

To help, I'm running a FREE online event on "How to…(insert event name), and I'd love to invite you as my guest.

What is the best way to send you details? LinkedIn message or email?

Kind regards

(First Name)

3. An Example to Add People to Your Email List:

Many thanks for accepting my connection request (First Name).

In my conversations with (Job Titles), I'm hearing (EMOTION 1) with (PAIN 1), some are (EMOTION 2) with (PAIN 2) and others are (EMOTION 3) with (PAIN 3).

To help, I've created a free guide with (insert what it contains).

What's the best way to send it to you? LinkedIn message or email?

Kind regards

(First Name)

4. An Example to Give a Demo or Taster Session Away For Free to Add Value:

Many thanks for connecting with me (First Name).

In my conversations with (Job Titles), I'm hearing (EMOTION 1) with (PAIN 1), some are (EMOTION 2) with (PAIN 2) and others are (EMOTION 3) with (PAIN 3).

To help you (insert what you are helping them with) I am selecting 3 (Job Titles) this month to receive a free (insert give away), which I normally charge £XXXX for. This is on a first-come, first served basis.

What week would suit you best to schedule this in?

Kind regards

(First Name)

These are simply some examples based on the various campaign types. We have written hundreds of campaign messages to help our clients with messages that drive a response from potential prospects.

As with any marketing campaigns, it's always best to test and measure, try different things until it works. If you aren't sure or need help, we provide consultation on outreach, and our P44 agency team run strategy sessions for clients who are looking for help with prospecting and outreach messages, on a 'done with you' basis. Get this right and it can make all the difference to your results.

5 ACTIONABLE INSIGHTS FROM THIS CHAPTER

1. Decide how many people per day you will invite to connect with you.

2. Choose the personalisation points you like and create template first messages.

3. Check out your followers and profile viewers that you have not yet connected with and get inviting the ones who look interesting to you and are a fit for your IDEAL client.

4. Set a target for invite to acceptance rate and decide how you will track it.

5. Write out your second messages for your chosen outreach campaign.

Chapter 7:
Observe the Masses, Do the Opposite

The title of this chapter is inspired by the late, great Walt Disney.

"Observe the Masses and do the Opposite"

is one of my favourite quotes and is a mantra I live by in both my business and my personal life.

This chapter is not for the feint-hearted(!!), but for those brave enough to embrace it you could secure a response rate of up to 40% from your prospecting efforts.

When I first train how to do this to both salespeople and business owners, I get a lot of push back. The people who love these methods are usually the super confident, extraverted personalities, who cannot wait to give it a go once they learn about these prospecting methods.

The people who take this on, try it and get it right get amazing results!

This chapter is about cutting through all that noise.

Remember how many prospecting messages are being received by decision makers? 5-10 on average a day, that's 25-50 a week, and 100-200 a month!

So how can you cut through the noise? How can you stand out from the crowd? How can you get someone to take notice of you?

The answer: Voice and Video Prospecting

Most people are full of fear, worried about how they will come across or use the excuse that culturally this just wouldn't work in their country. Well, believe me, I have heard every excuse going!

Moving your response rate when outbound prospecting from 3-8% up to 20-40% can make a huge difference to your pipeline and efficiency. Now I am not suggesting you use voice and video for every single new contact you make (although I do know people who do), I'd recommend keeping it for those contacts you really, really want a conversation with. The hard to reach, senior level decision-makers that sit in a boardroom, the ones who are targeted ALL the time.

Both video and voice messages are best sent using the LinkedIn® mobile app. I will explain both.

Voice Messaging

You do need to be connected to someone in order to send a voice note. Simply go to the messaging area of the mobile app, look to the right of the message and you will see a microphone icon.

Tap on the microphone and a big blue button appears, hold down to record and don't let go until you have finished speaking. If you make a mistake slide away to cancel it and you get an ask from LinkedIn to say are you sure you want to send? Just in case you need to re-record.

At the time of writing this book, voice messages are a maximum 60 seconds, which is plenty of time. I recommend making a prospecting message short and sweet and very in line with the second messages which I have already covered in the previous Chapter.

You'd be surprised how many people don't know this feature exists. I love using audio messages both for prospecting and also for people I am already in conversations with.

Video Messaging

There are a few ways to send a video message. You can simply click on the paperclip icon to the left of a message (in the LinkedIn® mobile app), which will reveal a whole menu of items. One of them is a video icon that says 'Take a video'.

This will immediately open the camera on your phone, you can record your video and choose to send once you are happy with it. Or another way (which is my preferred method) is to record a video as a pre-recorded message with subtitles and then send from your camera roll.

There are a couple of apps you can use for this: Apple Clips (iOs), AutoCap (Android) are my 'go to' apps, but you can find plenty of these types of apps in the Apple store or Google play store.

The way to send this through as a message is to choose the 'Send a Photo or Video' option from the attachment menu. Find your video, upload and send!

Hardly ANYONE uses videos for prospecting or messaging. They really do give the personal touch, especially if you use the person's name at the start so it doesn't make it look like you are blanket sending out the same message to everyone. Keep it short and sweet again, under 30 seconds if you can.

This will really help you to stand out from your competition, you will see a marked increase in response rate when using video messages.

Why not try it out! Send me a voice or video note saying you are in this Chapter and drop me a message telling me what you've learned so far from my book ☺.

ACTIONS FROM THIS CHAPTER

1. Practice sending a video message on LinkedIn®.

2. Practice sending a voice message to someone who has messaged you.

3. Send a prospecting video message to someone you don't know.

4. Send a prospecting voice message to someone you don't know.

5. Decide how many video/voice messages per week you will send out.

Chapter 8:
Lead Responses, What to Expect

When you start prospecting, or if you are already prospecting, you will come to realise that there are all sorts of different responses you may get in your inbox, ranging from zero response and being completely ignored, to 'let's book a call'.

It is important to set expectations on this, as everyone you meet and every reader who picked up this book will have a different definition of what a 'lead' is in their world. In fact, it's a common debate and conversation we need to have with every client we work with.

I ran a poll on LinkedIn a few months ago asking people to pick from the following to identify which one of these is a lead?

1. Not right now, contact me in 6 months
2. We've already got it covered
3. Don't try and sell me something

They are ultimately ALL leads, but an overwhelming 73% of people in the poll choosing option one. It is possible with the right sales and conversational skills to turn every response into a conversation with the human being on the other side of the inbox. In fact, most of our best clients have come from the 'don't try and sell me something response'. It usually turns into some banter and humour and light-hearted conversation and then from that a relationship is formed.

Let's now look at all the different response types you should expect and how to deal with them.

No Response to Second Message / Message Ignored

This is going to be the largest proportion of the reactions to your outreach, anywhere from 92-96% of your messages are not going to get a response. Expect this and know that, just because you don't get a response to a second message, the person has accepted you into their network and they will start to see you in their newsfeed if you post consistently. In fact, for the first 7 days after you have connected, you will see their posts and they will see yours. You can nurture these people by building your personal brand, by building both your visibility and credibility through your content.

These are the people I recommend re-targeting 3-6 months after they initially accept your connection request. They may not respond to your first outreach, mainly because they don't know, like or trust you yet, but after 6 months things may have changed, they may have different pain points, their buying window may now be open whereas it was not before. You could initially approach with one campaign type and then go again later with another campaign type. Eg. You could start with a value add campaign and then later target these people to invite them to an event.

We've Got It Covered / No Thanks / We Don't Need It

This could be for a number of reasons. So when you reply, ask a question, why is it a no? Have they covered this internally? Are they using another provider to fix this problem?

This is a lead but not for right now, if they are doing it themselves, there may be an opening in the future. If they are using another provider, there will be a contract end date. Do they want to be removed from your list or is it worth keeping in touch? Most people are quite happy to stay in touch, and don't forget, they may also change roles, move company and if they are open to keeping in touch, it could imply there is a future buying window or they aren't necessarily that happy with their current solution.

Not Right Now / Not Yet / Contact me in (X) Months

If you get this response, ask more questions. You could ask…

What's needs to have changed for the outcome to be different?
Why are they saying this? Is it because they are tied into contract or something else?

Always make sure you are taking notes and entering follow up details into your CRM. The amount of prospects who agree to being contacted again in 3 months, 6 months who then never hear from the salesperson again is shocking. Imagine if you or your team actually followed up when you said you were going to follow up.

I'm Not the Right Person, You Should Speak With (Name)

This is a good one, a referral to someone else in the organisation. Again, ask great questions. Can you mention their name & that you've spoken? Where would they guess it is on their agenda? Try to gain some insight before you approach the person they believe your solution is better for. Connect with them on LinkedIn and reference the conversation you have had with them (if you have permission to do so).

Don't Try and Sell me Something

The one everyone dreads. A negative response. Sometimes you just message people on a bad day, you could be the 11th prospecting message they've had that morning!

Find out, be vulnerable, fall back and ask them. I'm sorry, How many terrible pitches have you already had this morning? If you have used pain points, ask, would it be fair to say none of the points above are familiar? If you have used a 1-10 question, are they confident in their current approach or are they the wrong person?

I remember us having a conversation with the EMEA Sales Director of a large consulting firm, he replied 'Don't try and sell me something" to which we replied, "Am I the 10th person to pitch you today?", he replied, "No, the 11th" with a smiling emoji. We played on his ego, went vulnerable and asked for his help. "Just so I know for next time, what would I have to do differently to get your attention?", and so he went into mentoring mode, started to coach and help and a relationship formed. Then after an exchange of a few more messages, he then revealed that actually although it was the 11th prospecting message, he had received that day, that ours had stood out, and he actually needed help with social selling. Within 6 weeks he became a customer, and we added a very nice logo to our client list.

I'll Be in Touch

The ultimate in 'thanks but no thanks'. Again use questions here to determine if they are being genuine with that response. When are they expecting that will be? Is it worth re-reaching out in 3 months if I don't hear back from you? Most prospects don't expect you to, so they will usually say, 'sure, get back in touch in a few months'.

As mentioned before, most sales people don't follow up or enter leads like this into their CRM, but imagine if you did, or your team did. That you actually follow up when you say you are going to. That on its own will impress any prospect.

In the meantime, with the right approach to content (more on that later), you will have been showing up consistently in their newsfeed, nurturing and seeding more about how you can help them. Your next outreach may be better received.

It's still a response, and it's still an opportunity for a conversation. Remember, people move jobs all the time. The positive here is that they still connected with you, and they are still open to a conversation in the future. They may not have a need in their current role, but if they move up or into another company, who knows where it could go.

I Resonate With Your Message & I'm ready to talk

Now this doesn't happen often, but sometimes you prospect someone at the right time, with the right problem that you can solve and they are open to a conversation. Depending on the campaign type you are running, this could mean that they are happy to attend your event, or want to take you up on your high value offer, or want to download your email/lead magnet or they may want to move to a call.

Great! Move them to the first stage of your sales process. For me, when I am prospecting corporate and enterprise clients, that's usually a Discovery Call. For you it may be different. I use Calendly (http://calendly.com) for booking my appointments. It links to my diary and only shows prospects the dates and times that I am available. I also take advantage of the paid version so it's branded and looks professional, but more importantly, I can ask up to 10 questions about the prospect when they book a call.

If you want to see an example, go to this link and you don't actually need to book a call in order to see the questions:

http://calendly.com/pipeline44/discovery

That way I am better prepared for the meeting. More on preparing for meetings later and how to use LinkedIn® and Sales Navigator for research purposes.

Nurturing Leads

All of these leads, regardless of the response will need to go through your nurturing cadence. Whether this be through content on LinkedIn®, moving people with permission to your email list, sharing articles, adding value etc. Depending on the size of company you are working with, your Marketing department may already have a solid nurturing cadence in place for leads that are not ready to talk yet. If you are a smaller business and don't have a process for this yet, it's important to think about how you will nurture these people in the future.

If you are a Sales Navigator™ user, then I recommend moving these prospects that you have engaged in conversation with, into a 'Nurture' saved leads list, so that you can continue to get alerts on them, see the content they post so you can engage with their posts in the future and stay up to date with any career changes. I will cover more on Sales Navigator™ later in a number of chapters.

The main point here is that every conversation you have 1:1 in your inbox should be considered a lead. Most are at the 1% stage, but they are still people you have had a conversation with. You are now on their radar, and they on yours. Too many people dismiss these lead responses as dead ends, but handled the right way, with the right questions and the right follow up they can become future pipeline opportunities.

ACTIONS FROM THIS CHAPTER

1. Set your expectations, be OK with not every response being a positive one.

2. Ensure you have a proper nurture cadence in place for the 95-98% of people who are not in the buying window right now.

3. Set up some template responses for each type of lead response. Be prepared so that you can be efficient.

4. Read the book 'Asking Questions the Sandler Way' by Antonio Garrido

5. If you have Sales Navigator™ create a saved list called 'Prospects to Nurture'

55

Chapter 9:
Introduction to Sales Navigator

Everything in this book so far has been written for the FREE version of LinkedIn®. This chapter will help you determine if paying for LinkedIn's sales solutions is right for you and your business. There are several paid options to choose from on LinkedIn®. It helps to understand the breadth of the LinkedIn® offering; each is targeted at users in different situations:

Recruiters: The LinkedIn® Recruiter Lite and Recruiter Corporate are essential tools for recruiters. I've not met a true recruiter who does not subscribe to the LinkedIn® Recruiter offering. Having spent 13 years in the recruitment industry, these are premium products. Most of the agencies I work with, as well as corporate clients, have these solutions.

Job Seekers: If recruiters find the tools valuable, similarly, so do job seekers. The Job Seeker licence allows you to be seen as a featured applicant, compare yourself to other candidates, and send messages directly to recruiters. You'll also see everyone who has viewed your profile.

Professionals: The four levels for general use are (1) Free, (2) Premium, (3) Sales Navigator™ Core (4) Sales Navigator™ Advanced.

The major difference here is how deeply and with how much detail you can see your extended network, your ability to outreach to a wider network as well as the search functions, which give greater granularity than the free version. I have already covered the free version at length, so what do you get if you decide to upgrade?

LinkedIn® Premium Offering

Premium for business includes 15 InMail messages, advanced search filters, unlimited searches in your extended network and additional company data. Personally, I would suggest that if you are going to pay for LinkedIn®, that premium is NOT the option to go for.

I would always recommend Sales Navigator™ because for an extra $20 / £20 a month, you move from a basic car to a Formula One driving machine that will catapult your sales results to the next level IF you apply what I share in this book about prospecting and content.

LinkedIn® Sales Navigator Core Offering (For Individuals)

"Sales Navigator™ allows sales professionals to tap into the power of LinkedIn® efficiently. It improves social selling in support of powerful daily habits,"

Diana Kucer, Director of Global Product Marketing at LinkedIn® Corporation

Besides making it really easy for you to get connected with prospects and plan out a list of ideal connections, it can do a lot more for your business. If you have had the time to check LinkedIn® Sales Navigator™, you would have read their tagline, which correctly explains the motive of social selling and the navigator itself.

The tag line says, 'You know the art of selling. We can help with the science'. It is not just hit and trial method or cold calling tactics that run this amazing tool. It has sophisticated background algorithms; to give you lead recommendations which are customised as per your business needs and prospect profiles.

Sales Navigator is a social selling offering from LinkedIn® that can have an immediate and dramatic impact on results for most businesses. It allows you to find hidden decision makers at large accounts and engage with them based on their LinkedIn® activity.

There Are Two Options Available:

Sales Navigator™ Core (For Individuals)

Sales Navigator™ Advanced (For Teams)

Sales Navigator Features

Here is a list of all the features included with Sales Navigator™ Core offering:

- Easily find new and promising leads with advanced search options

- **Get real-time sales updates about your prospects and customers**

- Unlock full profiles for leads who aren't in your network

- See who has shown interest in your products and services, view their profiles

- Reach out to other members with InMail option

- Measure and track your social selling efforts with Social Selling Index (SSI) dashboard

- Build trusted relationships with colleagues and other members

- Reach out to different verticals and professionals across the globe

- Cross selling benefits to accompany your products and services

- Focus on the right people, reach them at the most appropriate time of selling

- **Unlimited search results with additional filters such as postcode and headcount**

- **The ability to save leads (people) and track their activity**

- **The ability to save accounts (companies) and track their activity**

- **'View Similar 'will give you an additional 100 suggested profiles**

- **Account Mapping tool allows you to see a helicopter view of the organisation, across multiple tiers**

- Get amazing insights on the go with mobile app availability

- **Create and save lists based on your Boolean searches**

The features in bold are my absolute favourites. If you have ever hit the commercial search limit on LinkedIn®, you will love that you can run unlimited searches. If you work very regionally specific, then you will love being able to search within a 10-15 mile radius of a specific postcode for example.

If you only want to prospect large companies, then you will love the fact that you can filter by size of company based on their headcount and the Account Mapping tool. If you are prospecting heavily, then you will adore the saved lists, meaning you can just jump back in and start prospecting again without having to re-type in your Boolean searches.

Sales Navigator™ Advanced Edition (For Sales Teams)

For those reading this from larger companies, Sales Navigator™ also comes in a multi-seat version; Sales Navigator™ Advanced for Sales Teams offers the following features:

- Find and contact anyone
- Sales Navigator InMail credits **50 per month**
- Leverage your team's network with TeamLink
- See Who's Viewed Your Profile from the last 90 days
- Open Profile

- Unlimited People Browsing
- Custom lead and account lists
- Advanced lead search and account search
- 10,000 saved leads per person
- Lead recommendations and saved leads
- Shareable custom lead and account lists
- Centralised Account Management
- Upload and manage your book of business
- Team collaboration tools
- Buyer Interest Alerts
- Exclusive insights to get ahead including real-time alerts on your leads and accounts
- Send Smart Links and track engagement
- Centralised billing for contracts sold through LinkedIn corporate sales (Volume and multi-year discounts, invoicing, dedicated relationship manager)
- Enterprise tools SSO, Employee Data Integration
- CRM Sync: Auto-Save, Activity Writeback, & ROI Reporting for Salesforce and Microsoft Dynamics 365 Sales (only available with Advanced Plus version)
- Advanced CRM integrations: Data Validation & Contact Creation for Salesforce and Microsoft Dynamics 365 Sales (only available with Advanced Plus version)

Many of my Corporate Clients have the Sales Navigator™ Advanced Team edition, and for a sales organisation, it can be a great way to motivate and drive competition, leveraging the SSI leaderboard as long as the team are fully trained in how to use it effectively.

Enterprise sales of LinkedIn® Sales Navigator are handled by Account Managers at LinkedIn Corporation headquarters, and prices will depend on the total number of licences and how good your negotiating skills are.

If you would like to be connected to a local LinkedIn® Account Manager from my network, please drop me a message on LinkedIn, and I would be happy to make a personal introduction. I am connected globally with Enterprise Account Managers.

If you want to enable your Sales Team to actually get results from your existing Sales Navigator™ investment, then contact me on LinkedIn® or drop an email to my team on hello@pipeline44.com.

Sales Navigator 30-Day Free Trial

You can get a free trial for one month to test it out for yourself. This demonstrates how confident the company is that Sales Navigator can have a tangible impact on your business.

A word of warning, when you first sign up, LinkedIn® will ask for your credit card details and will automatically select the annual plan, which means if you forget to cancel or don't want to continue with the trial, your card will be swiped for the full annual amount. So be sure to change it to the monthly plan if you want to pay monthly. You can cancel at any time and are not tied in for any length of time.

If you have previously taken a trial, you will have to wait a full 12 months to be able to take a trial again.

I do recommend taking a trial of the Sales Navigator tool, but only once you truly understand the free version. You can get results as a free user, but you will speed up the process and be more efficient with your time as a Sales Navigator licence holder.

I deliver deep-dive Sales Navigator™ training both in-house for corporate clients as well as in my Social Selling Academy for individuals. To learn more, drop me a message on LinkedIn® or send an email to sam@pipeline44.com.

More Information:

You can access the sales pages about LinkedIn® Sales Navigator™ and their new product Sales Insights here: https://business.linkedin.com/sales-solutions

You can compare plans here: https://business.linkedin.com/sales-solutions/compare-plans

5 ACTIONS FROM THIS CHAPTER

1. Take the 30-day free trial of Sales Navigator if you want to try it out.
2. Look at the different options depending on your role in your business.
3. Decide if you want to become a long-term Sales Navigator licence holder
4. Read the next few chapters to fully understand how to unlock Sales Navigator
5. Get trained in how to use it properly

Chapter 10:
Sales Navigator™ – Advanced Search

Sales Navigator™ is a phenomenal tool for finding your IDEAL client, so I recommend that as you go through this chapter, that you have your IDEAL client framework nearby or at least top of mind.

Before going into detail on specific searches within Sales Navigator™, there is some terminology you need to be aware of in the Sales Navigator environment that will help differentiate between people and companies.

Within Sales Navigator™ a 'Lead' is a person, and an 'Account' is a company. So, you can run searches for Leads and searches for Accounts. I will be using these terms throughout this chapter and subsequent chapters.

The better you can get at searches in the Sales Navigator™ environment, the more time efficient you will become. There are many filters you can take advantage of to really narrow down who or what you are looking for.

What I love about Sales Navigator™ is that you can save each search that you create, unlike the free LinkedIn environment. So you can set up a search once, find some good leads and as your network grows, these saved searches keep turning up more and more leads that match what you are looking for.

You can save both 'Lead' searches and 'Account' searches. There are 30 filters currently available for you to filter your 'Lead' searches and 15 available for your 'Account' searches. In addition to this you can utilise the search box to add additional keywords.

Lead Search Filters

The filters for 'Lead' searches currently include the following:

Company Filters
Company headcount
Current Company
Past Company
Company Type
Company Headquarters location

Role Filters
Current Job Title
Past Job Title

Function

Seniority Level

Years in Current Company

Years in Current Position

Buyer Intent Filters

Account has buyer intent (this is based on Company Page and advert interaction)

Spotlights Filter

Shared Activities and/or Shared Experiences

Posted Content

Keyword in Articles

Personal Filters

Connection Level (1st, 2nd, 3rd degree)

Geography

Industry

Years of Experience

Connections of (insert a connection name)

Groups

First Name

Last Name

Profile Language

TeamLink connections (only for Advanced and Enterprise Editions)

School Attended

Workflow Filters

Lead Lists

People in CRM (if connected Advanced and Enterprise Editions only)

Account Lists

People You Interacted With

Saved Leads and Accounts

This will make more sense when you go to Sales Navigator and create a new 'Lead 'search. You are presented with all of the filters on the left-hand side. You can drop down each as a menu and select from a menu or in some cases you can type in and options will show up for you.

Here is a screenshot from the time of writing this book, although I don't like to include too many as the user interface of LinkedIn and Sales Navigator can change so frequently.

Image: Sales Navigator Lead Search Filters

Lead	Account		‹ Collapse
0 filters applied			📌 Pin filters

Company

Company headcount 📌	+	Connection 📌	+
Current Company	+	Geography 📌	+
Past Company	+	Industry 📌	+
Company type	+	Years of experience 📌	+
Company headquarters	+	Connections of	+

Personal

Role

		Groups	+
Current job title 📌	+	First Name	+
Past job title 📌	+	Last Name	+
Function	+	Profile language	+
Seniority level	+	TeamLink connections of	+
Years in current company	+	School	+
Years in current position	+		

Buyer Intent

Workflow

		Lead lists 📌	+
Account has buyer intent ⑦	⬤	People in CRM 📌	+
		To enable filter, upgrade contract	

Spotlights

		Account lists	+
Activities and shared experiences 📌	+	People you interacted with	+

Posted Content

		Saved leads and accounts	+
Keyword in articles	+		

Copyright Pipeline 44 Group Limited 2023

Account Search Filters

The filters for 'Lead' searches currently include the following:

Company Filters

Annual revenue

Company headcount

Company headcount growth (by department)

Headquarters location

Industry

Number of Company PageFollowers

Department headcount (by function)

Department headcount growth (by function)

Fortune (if publicly listed)

Other Filters

Technologies used

Job opportunities

Recent activities

Buyer intent

Workflow Filters

Companies in CRM

Saved accounts

As with the lead searches, this will make much more sense when you go to Sales Navigator and create a new 'Account' search. You are presented with all of these filters on the left-hand side. You can drop down each as a menu and select from a menu or in some cases you can type in and options will show up for you.

There have been some great new additions recently to company filters and I find a lot of them to be very useful. For example, I look for companies where their sales department has seen significant headcount growth, and where they are using specific technologies.

It is worth going through both the 'Lead' and 'Account' filters, expanding them all to see what's there to get more familiar.

For example, there are now 460 industries available in the industry list on Sales Navigator. So being aware of what they are is helpful and fully understanding what to include in a search will help you to be more specific.

Here is a screenshot of the Account Filters from the time of writing this book:

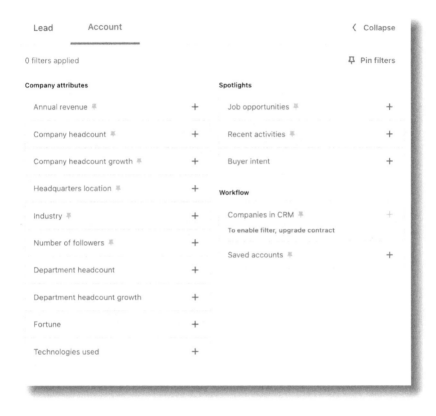

In the next chapter we will look at list building and how to save these new 'Leads' and 'Accounts' into the Sales Navigator environment, but for now have a go at running relevant searches based on your IDEAL client. Practice saving your searches, set different searches up for your different target markets.

ACTIONS FROM THIS CHAPTER

1. Run a search for 'Leads' that match your IDEAL client.

2. Run a search for 'Accounts' that match your IDEAL client.

3. Save searches that you know you are going to return to time and time again.

4. Go through each of the filters in 'Leads' searches and familiarise yourself.

5. Go through each of the filters in 'Accounts' searches and familiarise yourself.

Chapter 11:
Sales Navigator™ – List Building

List building is a core social selling activity, it's the most vital monthly habit to build and sets you up for prospecting success. The previous chapter will help you increase the quality of your lists to match your IDEAL client, this chapter will help to provide you with the right quantity of saved leads and accounts to make the time you invest in Sales Navigator™ efficient and worthwhile.

If you plan to prospect 20 people a day, you will need a list of 400 leads saved each month to give you enough to be able to prospect at this volume. If you plan to prospect 10 people a day you will need a list of 200 leads saved each month for you to prospect this many people.

I recommend blocking out up to 2 hours a month in your calendar at the start of a new month, to solely focus on list-building. If you use your saved searches correctly and continue to build your network you should find new leads being added each month regardless into your saved searches, then the rest you can find through new searches and going after different areas of your IDEAL client target market.

You can create 2 types of lists in Sales Navigator™, a 'Lead List' and an 'Account List'. Remember lead lists are lists of people, account lists are lists of companies.

There are a number of lists I recommend that you create inside your personal Sales Navigator™ account. Let's look at what they are, and then go into each in more detail. The lists you need to create are:

- A Top 100 hitlist of your priority key target accounts
- A list of all of your existing customers
- A list of all of your existing prospects in your sales pipeline
- A list of all of your key accounts that you want to expand
- A list of all of your Key Accounts that you want to recapture
- A list of the Accounts that you want to acquire as new Customers
- A list of all industry influencers, stakeholders and key people in your network

A Top 100 Hit List (Account List)

We've all got a dream logo we want to land, a set of companies that if you could just get them on your client list, they would change your business for the better. This hit list should be a priority list to build inside Sales Navigator™. If you don't have this list then create one! This list can be built using the filters and advanced search methods you learned in the previous chapter. Identify them, put them in a list and then you can monitor all of their activity and identify opportunities.

A list of All Your Existing Customers (Lead List)

Creating a list of all of your existing customers means that you can exclude them from your new list building making sure that you don't prospect a company you are already working with. You can also see what they are up to, get visibility on their posts and get alerts about them by building a list. More on that in Chapter 13. If your Sales Navigator™ is linked to your CRM then you will be able to see any Accounts or Leads that are already in your CRM as the two are connected.

If you use Salesforce or Microsoft Dynamics for example, you will be able to see people and companies that already exist in your CRM. Exclusions can be just as important as inclusions on Sales Navigator™, this will help you to build lists faster without worrying about targeting your existing customers.

As you close prospects into becoming customers, be sure to move them into your Customer list so that there is no confusion.

A List of All Your Existing Prospects in Your Sales Pipeline (Lead List and Account List)

Even if you haven't closed them yet, having your warm and hot prospects in a list in Sales Navigator™ means you can get alerted to content, posts, activities and trends happening in those companies. When I am in negotiations with a potential client or I have a new prospect on my radar, I add them to my saved lists for prospects. I add the company to a Saved Accounts list for prospects, and I make it a priority account on my Sales Navigator™ home newsfeed, so that I can see everything that is happening in that business. I add the people I am dealing with in the company to my Saved Leads lists, to help me close the deal and get a helicopter view on the Account. I also use Account Mapping for this which is covered in Chapter 12.

A List of Key Accounts You Want to Expand (Account List)

There may be some larger enterprise accounts that are already customers of yours, that you want to increase business with through expansion, either into other departments or other geographies. These are companies where you already have some business coming your way, but you know there could be more. These Accounts should exist on both your Existing Customer list and a list called 'Expand'. There won't be many, depending on your role, but if you are in Account Management rather than pure business development, this will be one of your most important lists.

A List of Key Accounts You Want to Recapture (Account List)

This won't be the biggest list you build, but on occasion we lose customers to a competitor, especially if you work in a business with lengthy contracts, where deals are done for 3-5 years. This list would be filled with the accounts that you have lost, and at some stage in the future you want to recapture and win them back again. This may not be relevant to everyone reading this book, but an important list to consider especially if you work in enterprise sales.

A List of Accounts For Acquisition, New Target Customers (Lead List and Account List)

This will be by far one of the biggest set of lists that you build, and I expect you will have multiple acquisition lists. Ranging from industry sector, to job functions and locations. If you are reading this and you have multiple target markets, each will need its own list to be built. You will need to build Account Lists with the Company names and you will also need to build Lead Lists with the specific people and roles you want to target in each account.

A List of Industry Influencers, Key Stakeholders & Thought Leaders (Lead List)

This list is optional but recommended. It's important to stay up to date with trends, industry news, opinions and what's happening in your world. By building a list of influencers, stakeholders and thought leaders, you can stay on top of things, get ideas for content, and get visible with influencers in your industry.

System Recommended Leads

There is one more list type to make you aware of, and that is the lists that Sales Navigator™ automatically creates for you. These are system generated based on what it calls 'recommended leads' and if you have your CRM connected via Sales Navigator™ you may also see some leads appear in lists based on your CRM system.

I can't express enough the importance of list building as a core habit to build. The better you get at this, the more you practice the easier it will become and the faster you will get at it. You can either manually save Accounts and Leads out or if you are happy with every person or company in your searches you can save time by choosing 'Select All' and then adding 25 at a time into lists.

To make your life easier when you are prospecting create lists into groups that make sense. For example, if you are going to send messages to Finance Leaders, don't create a list of Finance Leaders that also has a mixture of HR people and CEO's in the list. You want to be able to create a list and then ensure that the messages you are sending to those people all match up, and that you are not wasting time having to jump around to different 1st and 2nd messages.

You want to be able to create a list of 200-400 leads of all the same type of people and then every day you can go into your list, send out your 10, 15 or 20 invites and get on with the rest of your day. We will go into more detail on this in the fnal chapter when I give you your daily, weekly and monthly habits, setting this up in the right way now will save you time in the long run.

ACTIONS FROM THIS CHAPTER

1. Create your 'Top 100' hit list of key accounts and logos you want to land.

2. Build a list of 200-400 'Leads' to match your IDEAL client to prepare yourself for the month ahead of prospecting.

3. Put 'List Building' into your calendar as a monthly recurring event. You will need to dedicate at least 2 hours a month to this activity (or 30 mins a week, however you prefer to work).

4. Set up all of the separate lists mentioned in this chapter. Include prospects in your pipeline, accounts you want to expand and recapture, your existing customers and industry influencers.

5. Create saved lists in both 'Account Lists' and 'Lead Lists' for all of the different types of prospects you want to acquire, as new customers.

Chapter 12:
Sales Navigator - Account Mapping

Now that you have your Account lists built full of the companies you want to target, it's time to start exploring one of my favourite features of Sales Navigator™, account mapping. This is a relatively new feature only introduced in 2021, and is highly useful, especially if you are prospecting companies with 100+ employees, where you may need to speak with and influence multiple decision makers in the buying process.

What is an Account Map?

An Account Map is the process of visually representing the data points and the relationship dynamics at a prospect company. It's used by salespeople to get an overview of how an organisation functions, and helps you to identify the key decision-makers within your IDEAL client, key accounts.

In contrast to a typical organisational chart, an account map also takes the informal hierarchies into account to arrive at the 'best path of sale'. Account maps are available in some CRM systems, but you would need to know who all the key players are to build one in your CRM. By using the Sales Navigator™ account mapping tool, you may come across prospects and roles that you didn't know existed that may affect the buying process.

A well-constructed account map gives you a holistic, helicopter view of your prospects and customers. When you know who influences and controls budgets, you can build professional relationships with the stakeholders that matter. There are typically 8-12 people involved in a budget sign off in larger organisations, there is nothing worse than thinking you are going to close the deal and from out of nowhere, someone you weren't aware of comes in late to the process and puts a blocker on the deal or wants to make you work harder for the sale.

In Sales Navigator™ you can build multiple account maps for one key account. So, for example you can build one account map of the Sales & Marketing department, then you could also build another account map of the Operations, Legal, HR and departments. It really depends on what you are selling and how many departments your solution impacts.

There are three Tiers in an Account Map on Sales Navigator™, they are simply called Tier 1, Tier 2 and Tier 3. It's up to you how you treat these layers in the Account Map.

My personal preference is to split these tiers by type of buyer:

Economic Buyers: Budget Holders, C-Suite roles, Key Decision Makers

Technical Buyers: Sponsors, Mid-Senior Management – Influencers of decision

User Buyers: People who will use your solution but don't influence decision

I put all Economic buyers into Tier 1, Technical buyers into Tier 2 and User buyers into Tier 3. As you add people into each tier, Sales Navigator saves these as Leads automatically.

You can move people up and down tier levels by dragging them around the Account Map. You can have up to 20 people in one Account Map, so you can't put everyone in, but you can create a second Account Map if you need to for the same Account.

Here is an example Account Map which I created when I was prospecting this scale-up tech, company and now, they are a client. Names are removed for privacy reasons.

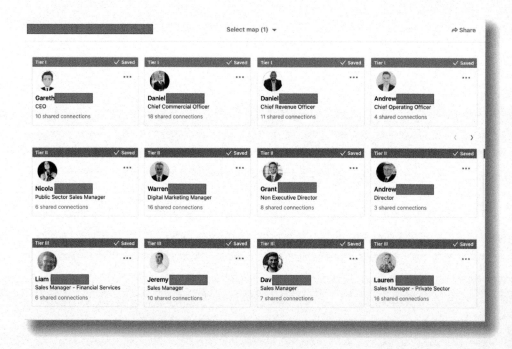

On the left as you are building your Account Map, you will see 'Recommended Leads' which Sales Navigator™ will suggest based on who you have already added into the map. You can also filter recommended leads by department. See image:

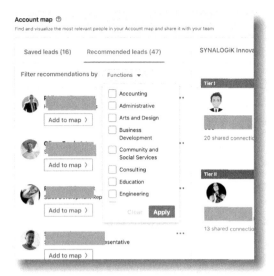

You can access account maps from each account page in Sales Navigator™. Find a company you want to prospect or already in the sales process with, search them up on Sales Navigator or find them from your saved account lists. Scroll down and you will see the account map underneath. You can remove any people/leads that are not correct and then move the right people in and save leads for those people who are not already captured in your saved leads list.

It can take some time to build an effective account map, 10-15 mins per account if you are doing it properly. I wouldn't recommend doing this for every single account you have saved, but there would be some priority ones to focus on. I would create an account map for:

- Your existing Key Accounts that you want to Expand
- Every prospect in your pipeline at 40% or higher prognosis
- Your Top 100 hit list – do 5 or 10 a week over time
- Key Customers where you only have a few contacts

Much like list-building, account mapping is a core skill to learn and practice. It will help you close bigger deals, convert more effectively and build better and stronger relationships with key accounts, those you already work with and those you want to work with. As you build out your account maps, be sure to connect with key stakeholders and invite them into your network.

The more touchpoints in the organisation you are prospecting the better. Especially if you also combine creating content on the newsfeed in your social selling habits. The more people in the prospect account who know who you are, see you as visible and credible, the better. You are likely to be up against competition, so getting to know everyone in the

73

decision-making process will be critical to your success. So many people potentially influence who the business goes to, do everything you can to make sure it's you and your business.

5 ACTIONABLE INSIGHTS FROM THIS CHAPTER

1. Create an Account Map for each of your existing Customers.

2. Create an Account Map for all prospects in your pipeline at 40% or above

3. Create an Account Map for your Top 100 target hit list (you have already built the list by now, create 10 Account Maps a week for 10 weeks and you are done).

4. Create an Account Map for the Key Accounts that you want to expand.

5. Practise creating multiple Account Maps with one account, using all Tiers and multiple departments.

Chapter 13:
Sales Navigator™ Newsfeed Engagement

What I love about the Sales Navigator™ home newsfeed is that there is no algorithm. Unlike the newsfeed on your LinkedIn.com feed, the only person in control of what you see, and who you see is you!

Your home newsfeed in Sales Navigator™ is driven by all of the work you have done to build saved lead lists and account lists. So if you create a list of prospects, or customers or target leads, you will start being alerted on the newsfeed about everything that is happening in those accounts and with those people.

So why is this important? When you are prospecting you need to have your finger on the pulse. Industry trends, changes in leadership, mergers and acquisitions, funding events, promotions, people changing roles and your prospects and customers being in the news can all positively or negatively affect deals you are working on. In addition, you need to be in the know if a key contact moves on or up in the organisation. By keeping an eye on the newsfeed, you can be alerted to key events. Another reason it's important to keep an eye on your newsfeed is so that you can do something I call 'intentional engagement'. If you have saved out 'Leads' (people) and 'Accounts' (companies) you will start to see what those people are posting on LinkedIn® showing up in your newsfeed.

Intentional Engagement

When you are on the normal LinkedIn® newsfeed, it's your activity and interactions with others and the algorithm that decides who and what you see. In Sales Navigator™ being able to see only the posts of the people in your saved lead lists is SO powerful. Most people on LinkedIn® like and comment on the posts of their mates, their colleagues, people they already know. This can be a good thing to do to support the people you like, but it won't win you business. It won't drive profile views and it won't drive inbound leads. Intentional engagement will. So what is it?

Intentional engagement is creating a habit of every day, logging into Sales Navigator™ to proactively find posts from your IDEAL client, and from your customers and prospects that you can add valuable insight to. Posts that you can react to, support their posts and most importantly create visibility with the person or company you are looking to work with.

Intentional engagement is important on the posts of your customers, the posts of your prospects in your pipeline and the posts of your IDEAL clients who don't yet know you exist. Even if you haven't added some of the people into your network yet, as long as you have saved them into an account list or lead list their posts will show in your newsfeed. A great strategy to increase acceptance rates with your prospects is to spend a week before you request the connection request actively liking and commenting on their posts. At the end of the day, everyone is craving attention and support on their content, and if you are regularly providing that to a prospect they will notice it. When you go to connect and add them as a new connection, they are more likely to connect with you because they will recognise your name and remember that you have recently interacted with them. I am not suggesting you do this with all prospects, but certainly the ones you really want to do business with, especially those in your Top 100 list.

Filtering What You See in the Newsfeed

When you log into Sales Navigator, you will see at the top of the home feed that it starts by showing you 'All Alerts'. You can then decide to to select whether you are looking at Account alerts from company pages, or Lead alerts which would be about the people in your saved lead lists.

So let's look at Lead Alerts first. You can choose to see them all or you can filter to show any of the following:
- Career Changes
- Lead Engagement
- Lead News
- Lead Shares
- Suggested Leads

Career changes will alert you to promotions in the same company as well as career moves where people move to another company. Use this as an opportunity to engage with that prospect, congratulate them and get visible on their post, you never know who else will see you and your comment on that post from inside or outside of your network. Make it a meaningful comment, not just 'Congrats!'.

Lead Engagement shows you which of your saved leads has viewed your profile, accepted a connection request for example.

Lead news, will show if any of your saved leads have been in the news or are trending, this is going to a small pool and is more relevant to Account alerts.

Lead shares, this is where you will spend most of your time when doing this 'intentional engagement'. Each morning I log into my Sales Navigator™, and I check the newsfeed for Lead Shares. Now not all of the people in your saved lead lists are going to be posting. In fact, only 3-5% of LinkedIn members actually post original content, but if you do see that they have posted, and it's a post you can add value to then it's worth spending a few minutes a day going down the most recent 'Lead Shares' to find posts that you can react and comment on.

You might be thinking, why bother? Well, there are plenty of reasons to bother, especially if you are in sales. When you interact with someone's post on the newsfeed you are training the LinkedIn® algorithm that you want to see more from them, and this works this other way too. If the prospect reacts to your comment, by replying or reacting to your comment, your posts are more likely to show up in their newsfeed in the future. So that's a big positive, you are massively increasing your visibility and credibility with someone who you want to do business with or are already prospecting. If you do this with existing customers, you are showing them your personal support, and this can help build the relationship further and create retention. If you are using intentional engagement on prospects in your pipeline you are keeping very top of mind with them. Your proposal might not be the highest thing on their priority list, but seeing you flagged as someone who has liked and/or commented on their post may give them the nudge that they need. The other reason to do this, and probably one of the most important is that when you comment or like a post, everyone else who has already engaged with that post will also see that you have done so. So let's say you have left a meaningful, insightful and useful comment on the post of a prospect. You are not only building visibility and credibility with the person you have interacted with, you are now also doing the same with everyone else that has also interacted with that post.

One of our agency clients recently started doing this, only a few minutes a day. She prospects CEOs of large, established companies. She saw the post of a CEO of a very well-known and well-respected brand in the UK. She left a lengthy and insightful comment on his post. That led to a conversation in her inbox, which led to a few conversations, which led to a meeting, which led to her landing him as a coaching client. If she had not used intentional engagement, she would never have been on his radar.

I have mentioned that your comments need to be meaningful, insightful and add value to the post. Ideally you would use at least 20 words, the lengthier the comment the higher the algorithm will position it in the list of comments, and the more likely your prospect will engage with the comment. I recommend using a question as part of your comment. Here is an example…

I recently engaged on the post of a prospect, it was a post about an event he had attended on culture and leadership. I congratulated him on the opportunity, said what a great event and venue it looked like and then asked the question, 'what were the top 3 lessons you learned from the other experts on the panel?'. He replied, answering my question and my visibility to the other people who had interacted with the post already and with the prospect himself grew significantly. This led to new profile views, and new connection requests from people of a similar stature and leadership level of my prospect. The main thing to remember when you are commenting on other people's posts is to never ever sell. Resist the opportunity to promote you or your company when you are commenting. Focus on giving value and building the relationship and you will get noticed and be remembered.

Now that we have looked at 'Lead Alerts', we will move on to 'Account Alerts'.

You can choose to see them all or you can filter to show a selection of the following:

- Account Growth
- Buyer Intent

- New Decision Makers
- Account News
- Account Updates
- Suggested Leads
- Account Risk

Most of these are fairly self-explanatory, so get familiar with the filters in your own Sales Navigator™. Buyer intent is driven by those people who have interacted with your paid ads and/or have visited your Company page. If you are in Sales you will find most of these Account alerts useful. I would recommend keeping all alerts on for Accounts. As well as seeing these in the newsfeed you can also see these by individual account when you go into each Account page inside Sales Navigator™. We will look at this in more detail in Chapter 15.

5 ACTIONABLE INSIGHTS FROM THIS CHAPTER

1. Go through your current Sales Navigator newsfeed and get familiar with all of the types of alerts available to you.

2. Use the filters at the top of the Sales Navigator newsfeed to show you specific updates, such as 'Lead Shares', 'Accounts in the News'.

3. Choose 5 posts created by prospects in your 'Saved Leads' lists to react/like and comment on their posts with something insightful (use at least 20 words).

4. Mark your calendar for 10 minutes at the start of every day, to engage on the Sales Navigator newsfeed. This will form part of your daily habits.

5. Pick out your Priority Accounts and mark the star on them, so that they show in the top right when you log in each day.

Chapter 14:
Sales Navigator – Smart Links

Smart Links, what are they and how can you leverage them?

These are my absolute favourite feature of Sales Navigator, however they are only available with the Advanced and Enterprise versions. So you may decide to upgrade your membership after this chapter. If you do great, if you don't that's OK too. Remember I don't work for LinkedIn®, I am an independent trainer, although I should probably be on commission for the upsells this chapter is going to generate!

A Smart Link is created in the Sales Navigator environment. It's a trackable link, creating a unique URL that can be used both inside and outside of the LinkedIn® environment. Anyone who clicks on a Smart Link has to approve that their viewing of the Smart Link will be traceable and the owner of the Smart Link will be privy to that information.

Inside a Smart Link you can upload multiple file types and add multiple links, including:

- A link to your calendar to book a call
- A link to any URL including specific web pages you want to direct people to
- Landing pages – which take people to your email list
- Files including PDFs, Word Documents, PowerPoint presentations, Excel Sheets
- Videos
- Images
- YouTube links
- Case Studies
- Event Registration Page
- Testimonials
- Sales Proposals
- Free Resources

You can add up to 15 items within one Smart Link, 15 is a lot, so I recommend not overwhelming your reader, 4-6 items inside one Smart Link is a good amount. It is also recommended to consider the different personality types who might be accessing the information, some readers will want the bullet points and high-level information only, others may want lots of detail.

The fantastic thing about a Smart Link is that you get notified who has accessed your Smart Link, then you can see how many items they spent time on as well as exactly how many minutes or seconds they spent on each one!

This image shows you what it looks like. This is taken from my Smart Link that promotes my Sales Navigator Masterclasses. I have included a PowerPoint presentation, a link to book a call, an image, a replay of a free workshop about Sales Navigator and the booking link for people to secure their place on an upcoming Masterclass:

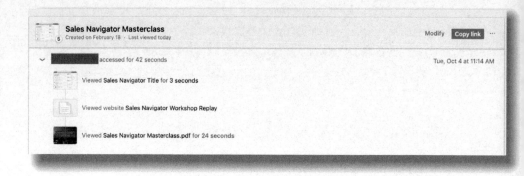

As a general rule, if someone has accessed my Smart Link for more than 30 seconds and has visited a number of the options within the Smart Link, I will drop that person a message on LinkedIn® with something like this:

Hi (First Name),

Many thanks for taking a look at the details of (insert topic of Smart Link).

I'm curious... what peaked your interest?

Sam

It's an open question, allowing them to respond openly, I don't launch into a sales pitch, only aim to start the conversation. Some visitors of your Smart Link will be brand new to you and many not already connected to you on LinkedIn.

In this chapter I will talk you through the many ways that I use Smart Links to drive warm and hot leads.

Smart Links used in LinkedIn® Posts

When you post content on LinkedIn, you have some idea of the analytics, in terms of who has viewed your post. The analytics will give you number of views, level of engagement and some very broad stats on the location, industry and seniority of the people who saw your post.

80

What I love about Smart Links, is when you embed a Smart Link into a LinkedIn post, you can actually see precisely who clicked through on your content. It's a great way of seeing all of the 'LinkedIn® lurkers' the people who follow you and love what you post, but never engage with your content!

A Smart Link is a LinkedIn link, starting with linkedin.com so it's not taking the reader away from the LinkedIn environment, so you are not impacted by the algorithm for including a link in your post. You won't get tons of engagement on your post, but if it was very specifically aimed content at a specific target IDEAL client, you can see who is engaging with your post, and how long they spent looking at the information.

I wouldn't recommend including a Smart Link in every single post, but I would recommend doing it once every 1-2 weeks. It can really be useful to know who is looking at the content you produce. My advice would be to make the Smart Link super helpful and of high perceived value to your audience.

Always ensure if you are putting out a Smart Link in your content, that the Smart Link contains the option to book a call with you and/or also includes a landing page to capture their email and move them into your nurture process for future marketing.

Smart Links Embedded into LinkedIn® Articles & Newsletters

If you, or your Company are producing Articles or Newsletters on LinkedIn® this is another great place to include one or multiple Smart Links, for all the reasons I mention above.

When you are giving massive value, helpful and advice and tips, it's OK to include links for people to find out more. So instead of sending people to your website, where you don't know who has visited, use a Smart Link instead. That way you can track who engages with the Smart Link and follow up in an appropriate way.

From a selfish perspective as a salesperson, if you send people to the Company website, yes they may go onto visit the website, fill out a web contact form (or not) and that lead once qualified may not end up back with you. By using Smart Links you are in control of the lead capture and lead follow-up. You can prove the lead originated from your activity and you own the commission on this prospect if they become a customer.

If you are not personally using the LinkedIn® Articles or Newsletter feature, why not be proactive and suggest to your marketing department that they start embedding your Smart Links inside company communications. Fully traceable and it's unlikely your marketing department have Sales Navigator licences, so they won't be able to create Smart Links themselves.

Smart Links in Your Newsletter or Blog or Website

Although Smart Links are created in the LinkedIn® environment, they create a unique URL that can be used anywhere outside of LinkedIn®. I highly recommend using them in your newsletter, blog or company website. You can get information about the numbers of people that have visited your website and you can tell who has opened your newsletter, but to be able to track and trace who has clicked on a Smart Link that has piqued their interest and be able to see how long they interacted with it and what they interacted with is super useful information.

Smart Links in Your LinkedIn® Profile

What an opportunity! Drive your profile viewers to a Smart Link or multiple Smart Links and you know exactly who your hot leads are. I recommend adding a couple of Smart Links to your profile 'Featured Section' and then also add one into your About section.

If you want to, you could also include one or two in your 'Work Experience' section where you can also upload media links. I have a link to my Sales Navigator Masterclasses on my profile as well as a link to free resources such as my podcast and free events, all in the same Smart Link as the place where people can access my book.

Smart Links in Your Email Footers

Not every company has these, but if you use them, why not add your Smart Link to your email footers. Every employee in your business is sending out emails. So include your core Smart Link that you want to drive people to on your email footers.

Smart Links for Your Sales Proposals

Finally, my favourite one. If you are in sales this is killer! Instead of sending your sales proposals or quotations in via email, send them as a Smart Link. If it goes as an email, you can't tell when it's been looked at, or how many times. You can't tell if it has been forwarded on or who else up the food chain is also looking at it, besides the people you have been speaking to.

I send all of my sales proposals and follow up documents as a Smart Link. I personalise it with a video as the first element in the Smart Link, I include a link to my Calendly in case they want to book a follow up meeting, and I include any documents, usually a slide deck and or a PDF with quotation that we have already agreed and discussed.

I can tell how hot a prospect is by how many times they have accessed it, and how long they have spent going through it. You can choose to make your documents downloadable or not, I usually make mine not downloadable so anyone who wants to look has to use the Smart Link to do so.

A recent prospect I sent a Smart Link proposal to, the VP of Sales for EMEA in a tech company, looked at the Smart

Link 25 times in a week. He and his colleague even accessed it 6 times on their weekends. That prospect is now a client and closed within 2 weeks of the initial conversation. If you are not using Smart Links in your sales process you are missing out on a huge opportunity to understand what's happening in the final stages of your pipeline.

In summary, Smart Links are just brilliant. I appreciate you may now be considering an upgrade to the Advanced version of Sales Navigator™ if you are only on the Core version, but it will be worth the investment if you use Smart Links correctly. If you already have them and are not taking advantage, make this a priority!

5 ACTIONABLE INSIGHTS FROM THIS CHAPTER

1. If you are on the Core version of LinkedIn and want Smart Links, then upgrade to the Advanced version so you can access this feature.

2. Set up a Smart Link for each of your Products and/or Services. Add the relevant ones to your LinkedIn profile in the 'Featured' Section.

3. Set up a Smart Link for larger size deal sales proposals. When you send to a client, send the Smart Link so you know how hot the prospect is and you can see who else has accessed the Smart Link in the company. Add these people to your Account Map.

4. Set up a Smart Link for your free resources, any useful links on your website, add your blogs, articles, podcast, white papers, case studies. Add a personal video into the Smart Link inviting people to look around.

5. Decide where in your marketing process you will use your Smart Links, based on the list of ideas I have provided for Smart Link usage.

Chapter 15:
Sales Navigator – Insights

Thinking back to the first chapter when you learned about the Social Selling Index (SSI Score), one of the scores is called 'Engage with Insights'. This is heavily linked, not solely linked, to your activity in Sales Navigator when it comes to insights.

Insights is relevant to Accounts in the Sales Navigator™ environment. For this chapter have one company in mind, ideally a company that is in your pipeline or is in your Top 100 hit list. Now go to that Account inside Sales Navigator™. You will find lots of useful information in there, relating to the company growth, headcount, employees by department and in there you will find a button that is called Insights.

These are similar to the alerts that come up on the newsfeed that you found out about in Chapter 13. You will find in the Insights tab information about:

- Employee count
- Distribution & headcount
- New hires
- Job openings

You will also see a section called 'People Also Viewed'. This will provide you with insights about other companies that might also match your IDEAL client based on the company you are currently viewing.

At the bottom of the Account page you will see specific insights about:
- Account Growth
- Account Risk
- Account News
- Account Updates
- New Decision Makers
- Career Changes
- Suggested Leads
- Buyer Intent

Buyer Intent is only available to customers who are on the Sales Navigator Advanced & Advanced Plus plans. When will you gain insights on Buyer intent? You will receive a Leadership Alert when a VP, CXO, Partner, or Owner at your saved Account views your LinkedIn company page or company website. You will also, receive an Employee Alert when someone from a saved Account, excluding leadership (VP, CXO, Partner, or Owner Level), views your LinkedIn

84

company page or company website. Alerts triggered by company website visits require the LinkedIn Insight Tag on your website. Learn more about Insight Tags here.

Note: Alerts display information on the attributes of the potential buyers, but LinkedIn® Corporation does not share individual information in order to protect buyer privacy.

In the next chapter you are going to learn about how you can use these insights in preparation for a sales meeting.

5 ACTIONABLE INSIGHTS FROM THIS CHAPTER

1. Look at the Insights of 5 Key Accounts from your Top 100 List.

2. Look at the Insights of 5 of your Existing Customers.

3. Check if your website has the LinkedIn insight tag so that you can get notified about Buyer Intent and Buyer Interest if you are on the Advanced or Advanced Plus version of Sales Navigator™.

4. Go to the 'People also Viewed' section of 5 Key Accounts see if you find anything useful.

5. Check in on your Green SSI Score in the Social Selling Index before you start delving into Insights, record it and watch it go up as you start using Insights more.

Chapter 16:
Preparing for Sales Meetings

Are you and your sales team winging it or winning it? In my experience, most are winging it. When I am preparing for a sales meeting with a Corporate or Enterprise client here is how I used Sales Navigator and LinkedIn® to prepare for the meeting. Now you have gone through the Sales Navigator™ chapters this will make more sense to you.

1. Account Mapping

I complete a full Account Map, using the Account Mapping tool inside Sales Navigator™, so I can see all key stakeholders, across 3 levels of decision makers. I visit the profiles of the leadership team and the sales and marketing teams I will be training.

2. Company Page

I look through the last 20 posts on the Company Page to ensure I am up to speed on the Company activity, wins and successes. I comment on the posts that have been re-shared by the leadership team. I follow their Company Page and saved the Account in Sales Navigator™ so I don't miss any future posts.

3. Saved Leads

I have saved the people I am dealing with in the sales process, as Saved Leads. This morning. when I logged into Sales Navigator™, I was alerted to the fact that they were shortlisted yesterday for a big award in their industry, something I can talk about in the meeting. Without Sales Navigator this would not have been on my radar.

4. Insights

I have used the Insights in Sales Navigator™ to look at their growth in headcount, revenue as well as hiring moves, they have made. I got some of this from previous meetings, but Sales Navigator is providing me with more. They've doubled revenue year on year throughout the last 3 years and have gone from a team of Co-Founders to over 60 employees in that same time.

5. Personality Profiling

I have used profiling tools to look at the personality profiles of the main decision makers, to help me understand their buying preferences and personality styles, so I can better understand how I need to show up in the sales meeting. More on that shortly.

6. Pre-Call Plan

I have created a full pre-call plan, I am prepared, I know what questions I need to ask, and I know what questions to expect.

Do your salespeople do all the above to prepare for a sales meeting? What difference would it make if they knew how to leverage all of the tools available to them to increase conversion rates?

Using LinkedIn® for People Research

LinkedIn® and Sales Navigator™ are phenomenal research tools. You can learn so much about a potential prospect just by doing some simple research on both them and the company they work for, which will increase the chances of you securing the business.

You can research the people you are meeting with, their senior leadership team and all people involved in the decision-making process. You can learn about the company's hiring pattern, see whether they are in growth or decline, learn what departments are growing, see their investment and funding history and understand ahead of the meeting what questions you can ask to discover if there is an opportunity for you.

Research Task

Pick someone you are due to meet in the next few weeks; someone you are prospecting or a new connection that is directly in your target market. Now visit their LinkedIn® and then answer these questions about them:

- How many mutual connections do you share?
- How many LinkedIn® followers do they have?

- Which School, College, or University did they attend?
- What education level did they achieve?
- Where are they based?
- Where have they previously worked? How long were they there?
- What Interests do they have?
- What groups do they belong to?
- What Influencers do they follow?
- What Companies do they follow?
- What types of content do they share?
- Who has recommended them?
- What voluntary causes or charities do they support?

Using LinkedIn® for Company Research

Now go to their current company, usually, you can find this in the 'Work Experience' section of their LinkedIn® profile. Click on the logo next to their job title, now answer these questions about the Company:

- Which Company do they represent?
- How many employees does the Company have?
- What Competitors are identified in the company's 'Also Viewed' section
- Are they hiring? If so, what roles are they advertising?
- If you have a premium or Sales Navigator account, go to 'Insights' for details of hiring trends and what departments are in growth or decline
- What type of content and posts are they putting out on their Company page?
- How many followers does the Company Page have?
- What key Products and Services do they highlight in their Company page?

Imagine being armed with all this information before a meeting? LinkedIn® gives you so much information, and this can be one of the best ways to build rapport in the early stages of a new business relationship. Use this research to find out what you have in common and look at topics you could bring into the conversation. It takes some time to do this properly, but it's well worth it especially when you combine it with the next section of this Chapter, being able to know their personality profile.

Crystal Knows

This is my favourite Chrome extension; I absolutely love it! Crystal Knows can tell you anyone's personality directly from their LinkedIn® Profile. It can help you to understand yourself better and improve your team, as well as prospect more effectively and close more deals.

Imagine going into a phone call or a sales meeting with a prospect, a decision maker you have never met before and actually understanding what makes them tick, how to speak with them, what to prepare and how to behave with them based on their detailed personality profile.

Welcome to Crystal Knows! You can visit their website and download the Chrome extension directly. There is also a mobile app version for using Crystal on the go. Get Crystal Knows Here. I share this amazing tool at my LinkedIn® Masterclasses and the amount of people who use it and then close deals because of their new knowledge about their prospects is astounding.

The free version gives you just 10 profiles in total, and then you need to move to a premium account which at the time of writing this starts from $59 per month on a recurring monthly subscription. In my opinion, this is an absolute bargain if you are in sales and choose to use it for each sales call or meeting.

How does it work?

Crystal analyses millions of data points to accurately identify anyone's personality. Crystal uses personality AI to accurately identify anyone's behavioural patterns by analysing text samples, assessment responses, and other attributes. As of 2022, Crystal profiles are 85% accurate. I always recommend using Crystal as a guideline, and this will give you a significant competitive advantage for closing more sales.

What Will You Do Differently?

So now that you are armed with more information on how you can prepare more effectively for sales meetings, what will you do differently? How will you prepare better the next time you are faced with a meeting with a prospect?

5 ACTIONABLE INSIGHTS FROM THIS CHAPTER

1. Use LinkedIn® and Sales Navigator™ to research information about each prospect you are going to sell to.

2. Use LinkedIn® and Sales Navigator™ to research company information to give you different insights.

3. Create a pre-call plan for an upcoming sales meeting.

4. Set up an Account Map for an upcoming meeting, adding all decision makers at each level of buyer.

5. Schedule out times in your diary before and after sales meetings, to prepare and debrief.

Chapter 17:
Easy content Themes for Salespeople

So far in this book, I have covered many ways in which you can engage in conversation with your target market, which will lead to sales opportunities. These are proactive tactics where you can generate leads in a mostly outbound way through LinkedIn® outreach and leveraging your new amazing LinkedIn® profile.

Now it's time to look at 'INBOUND lead generation'. Over the coming months and years, by applying the social selling strategies outlined in this book, you will be building up an incredible network of connections who match your IDEAL client. This chapter is all about content creation and posting with purpose.

Helping you to leverage the LinkedIn® newsfeed to explode your visibility and credibility in ways that you have never done before. When you get your content marketing right, you can build your personal brand, connect with your audience and get your LinkedIn® network to know, like and trust you.

Content is King

If you aren't posting content on LinkedIn®, you may as well be invisible. Content helps you to position yourself as an expert in what you do (more on that in Chapter 8). If you do post content well and with a focus on your exact target market, you will start to become known in your sector, and you will grow your connections and develop 'know, like and trust' of your personal brand. Everyone has heard the expression that 'Content is King'.

It absolutely is one of the best social selling strategies to drive inbound leads to your inbox on LinkedIn®. Almost every time I post on LinkedIn®, I get people sending me messages asking me how they can work with me. Approximately 3-5 leads inbound leads a day come into our business now as a result of social selling.

I set aside half a day a week for content creation, I am serious about being a dominant player globally, and in order to achieve my big mission to create £1billion in sales for my clients, I must put out great content to help my audience to become better at social selling through LinkedIn®.

This does not mean you need to spend that much time on content, but you do need to be planning it out and thinking about what kind of content you could create to build your company brand and your personal brand through the LinkedIn® newsfeed.

Connection is Queen

Content may be King, but it is not purely about quantity of content. It also needs to connect with your audience. I say connection is Queen. Always keep your target market top of mind when posting on LinkedIn®. Remember, your LinkedIn® profile is aimed at your IDEAL client. You are prospecting to build up your network of connections who match your IDEAL client. Now you can serve them with content that will educate, inspire and engage them. Over time as you build that connection with your audience, more of them will be attracted towards you, which will drive inbound leads.

The key factor here is authenticity. Be YOU! Don't try to be anyone else. You are never going to connect with every single part of your network. You will draw the people towards you and attract the people who you connect with and who will see you for who you really are. Real is the new fake. The rawer and more authentic your videos are, the better. You don't need a big production crew, and it does not need to be perfect. You are human. You will make mistakes. If you are recording a video, don't do 50 takes to get it perfectly right; go with the one that will connect best with your audience.

Engagement is Critical

Ever wondered why some of your posts receive hundreds or even thousands of views and others just simply fade into nonexistence like tumbleweed? Well, this is all to do with how much engagement your post receives. Early engagement on a post, particularly in the first 2 hours of a post going up, will determine the momentum of that post's penetration into your LinkedIn® network.

When you first put out a new piece of content on LinkedIn®, only 2-8% of your network see that post. In order for the LinkedIn® algorithm to kick into gear and start sharing that content with more and more people in your network, the post needs to have lots of engagement. This means any of the 6 types of LinkedIn® reactions to the post, quite a new feature, but a post can now receive a 'Like', a 'Love', a 'Celebrate', an 'Insightful', a 'Support' or 'Curious' reaction. In June 2022 LinkedIn also introduced a much awaited 'Funny' reaction.

People can 'Share' with their network, or 'Repost' or they can 'Comment' underneath the post. Preferably you want them to do all three or a combination of these responses. When they repost as well as benefiting from the impressions and engagements on your original post, you will also benefit from the interactions of the post from the person who reposted your content! Another new feature added by LinkedIn® in 2022.

The LinkedIn® algorithm loves comments. In fact it weights these the highest. So if your post receives a significant amount of comments, then more and more people will be exposed to that piece of content.

Each comment can be commented back on, so ensure that when you receive a comment, you respond by asking a question or driving a discussion. Comments upon comments will help to drive engagement. Ideally, use at least 20 words in a comment. The algorithm considers responses with 20+ words to be stronger engagement. Healthy debate and discussion under posts works really well.

Some key things to bear in mind when it comes to LinkedIn® content creation to maximise engagement:

- LinkedIn® wants you to create your own original content. Sharing other people's posts will help them, but it won't help you. Creating your own content will always drive more engagement and activity on your own posts.

- Avoid scheduling tools to push out content to your LinkedIn® newsfeed. You will be penalised for this in fewer views. LinkedIn® can tell when you have done this, and even worse in some cases, so can your connections. Always create the content natively from within LinkedIn®.

- Avoid posting links to external sites. LinkedIn® makes its money by keeping members within LinkedIn®, so it has more people to show ads to. When you post and send people away from LinkedIn®, don't expect the post to be seen by a lot of people. It would be better to post the link in the comments.

- Comments on posts need to be more than 20 words in length for LinkedIn® to consider these comments insightful engagement. So simply having people comment with 'Yes' or 'great post' isn't enough for the comments to be considered true engagement. The longer the comments are, the better. This is also the case with your own replies.

- An engaged view on a video is a minimum of 3 seconds. A view on other post types means it went across someone's newsfeed. Dwell time is important, so how long someone stayed on your post is critical. I will help you with this when we look at the 11 different types of posts you can create. You can now see detailed video viewing stats in the post analytics, including the number of views and the length of time people have viewed the video.

- As with every aspect of social selling, no pitching allowed! You will not get engagement on a post which is purely a sales pitch or an advert. Gary V says it best. **"People want to watch the TV show, not the commercials in between the TV show."** They want the story behind your journey and your brand, they love to buy, but they don't want to be sold. So avoid any 'call this number' or 'check out my website' or 'contact me' in the text or the video. People know how to reach you through LinkedIn®. Just don't repel them by selling in your content. Attract them!

Engagement is absolutely critical to your success in content visibility on the newsfeed. Don't expect engagement on your posts if you are not engaging on other people's posts. It's a 2 way street.

Measuring Post Impressions

Each time you post, you can see the number of impressions that post receives. There is a small graph at the bottom of each post. If you click that, you can see useful information and statistics such as which companies are viewing your post, the job titles that people hold who have viewed the post and which locations they are viewing from. A phenomenal tool that I recommend for analysing your LinkedIn metrics is SHIELD analytics. Learn more here: http://shieldapp.ai

Keep track of your post impressions and engagement, look at your highest viewed content and learn what worked and what didn't. LinkedIn® regularly changes the algorithm behind post views. Create great content, add value to your connections and engagement will happen. As your network of connections grows, combined with your own confidence in posting, so your post views will increase.

In March 2022, LinkedIn introduced better analytics which you can now access from your dashboard on your profile. It's in the same place as your profile views and search appearances.

You can look at your data from the last 7 days, 28 days, 90 days and 365 days, comparing impressions (this was previously called views) and engagement (reactions and comments). You can then break these down by industry, job title, location, seniority of role and more. Finally, some stronger analytics from LinkedIn®; good news for everyone!

15 Easy Content Themes for Salespeople

There are many different types of LinkedIn® posts and various different themes you can get ideas from. In my book "Linked Inbound" I talk about 20 different content themes, but for the purpose of this book which is mostly aimed at salespeople and sales leaders, I thought it would be better to give you the themes that are easiest for you, based on your role in the business.

As you read each one, think about how you could apply that theme to your day to day content plan.

1. Educational Posts

An educational post is designed to provide value, educate and give help, advice and tips to your target market. You have accumulated so much knowledge and expertise, and now it's time to share it. The more you give, the more will come back to you in return. Don't hold back; educate, add value and add even more value. You could share top tips, interview people, and create helpful videos, or 'how to' clips. Demonstrate your knowledge and share it with the LinkedIn® community. People are more likely to buy from you the more you give away.

This type of post is easy to create; simply brainstorm all of the topics you would consider yourself to be highly knowledgeable about. Now write down a list under each topic as sub-headings that could be mini-posts about that topic. Every sliver of information you have in your head is a LinkedIn® educational post. You could drip feed help, advice and tips for the next year about what you know if you just took the time to sit down and list out the knowledge you have.

A great book recommendation for you would be 'They Ask, You Answer' by Marcus Goldstein. He gives so many strategies on content creation simply by answering the questions that your prospects ask on a day to day basis when you are out selling. An absolutely amazing guide to content creation based on your customers.

Another great tool to use is Answer The Public. You can find this website using the following link: http://AnswerThePublic.com. Simply enter your specialist topic, and Answer The Public will give you hundreds of questions that the general public are typing into search engines. Start by answering them through your posts.

Educational posts are a great way to build your brand, position you as a 'go-to' expert and attract your ideal client towards you.

2. Gratitude Posts

Giving gratitude. Saying thank-you, is a great way to help others and thank people in your network for the great support that they have been to you. Use these types of posts on LinkedIn® to give gratitude, and tag them in the post so that they are notified.

This is an easy way to bring your brand into their network and to share with people that you give to others by saying thank you. When you give, you gain indirectly, so help others to gain exposure to your network, and you never know what will happen.

Make the post all about the other person, say why you are acknowledging them and suggest that if someone wants a personal introduction to your amazing business contact, they should message you directly.

One way you can thank others is by 'Giving Kudos'. Go to the person's LinkedIn® profile that you want to give some kudos to, click in the hidden (...) menu next to the blue message button and choose 'Give Kudos'. There are a number of different ways to thank someone in this way, including being a great mentor, being a team player, being an inspirational leader, and so many more. I love this feature if you are a business owner with a team or a manager in a large organisation. What a fantastic way to motivate employees by publicly giving them Kudos to your LinkedIn® network.

3. Documentary Posts

This is my absolute favourite type of post and is one of the themes that will drive the most inbound leads to your business when done well. A documentary post is simply sharing with your network what you are up to.

Now I am sure that most days, you are going about your business, doing what you do, not even thinking for a second about documenting it or sharing what you are doing with others. If you don't, you are missing a trick! This is one of the easiest ways to create posts that sell without selling. This year alone, this one theme has generated me in excess of £250,000 in new revenue by simply sharing what I am up to. Every time I speak on stage anywhere in the world, I post about it. Every time I deliver a LinkedIn® Masterclass, I post about it. Every time I deliver a workshop for a sales team, I post about it.

Every time I deliver a virtual presentation or record a podcast I post about it. Every time I secure a win for a client, I post about it!
You get the idea... pull back the curtains on your world.

Documenting what you are doing is social proof that you are out there doing what you do and getting results for your clients. The best way to think about this theme is to look back over your calendar for the last 7-14 days.

- Where have you been?

- What online events, in-person conferences or seminars have you attended?

- Who have you met with? Online or in-person.

- What results have you had achieved for your clients?

- What have you done personally?

- What have you done professionally?

- What have you learnt?

- What have you read or listened to?

All of these can be turned into LinkedIn® posts that simply document what you have been up to. When you master these documentary style posts, you will really be selling without selling. All it takes is for someone in your target market to see the post and inbox you saying "I've been following your posts on LinkedIn®' and for them to identify with what you have been doing to help others just like them.

You never know who is seeing your posts. You never know who in your extended network is going to see your posts. I recently won a new Corporate Client, a multi-billion ££ turnover company, who came to me because I was regularly sharing documentary style posts. One of my 1st degree connections was commenting on and liking my posts, and a Commercial Director, who I was not connected to in any way, reached out to me because one of their Sales Managers had been seeing me pop up in his newsfeed regularly delivering LinkedIn® Masterclasses and in-house training. When asked to recommend a Social Selling strategist and LinkedIn® expert, he named me, and I won the business.

4. Wins and Success Posts

A few years ago, I was delivering a Masterclass, and in the room, there was an expert in Oil & Gas recruitment. He had never posted on LinkedIn® before, and when we started talking about this theme, he could not believe that anyone would be remotely interested in what he was up to, his successes in business or how it could create him inbound leads. My Masterclasses are highly practical, so after I had taught the class the theory of content creation, we as a group all posted a piece of content on LinkedIn® together. He chose to create a post highlighting some success he had been having.

He shared in his first ever LinkedIn® post how he had successfully placed 3 senior level candidates in the Middle East in the Oil and Gas Industry in challenging roles that the client had been struggling to fill, and how the clients were over the moon and it had led to him having his best quarter ever. Now due to the confidential nature of his work, he could not mention the name of the companies or the candidates he had placed. But nevertheless, it was a great post designed to tap into a prospect's pain points and demonstrate his expertise in his niche.

The Masterclass delegates helped his post by commenting to get some engagement quickly. They all do that for each other in the classroom. Within 2 hours of the post going live, Mark had received an inbound lead from an old contact of his who he had worked with 7 years prior. He had not realised that he had set up his own business, and he resonated with the post because he had been struggling to fill some challenging roles himself in the oil and gas sector. He walked out of the Masterclass with a meeting and 3 new vacancies to work on. He couldn't believe it!

So the lesson here is: share your wins and successes. The LinkedIn® ecosystem is a supportive place where people will follow your journey and celebrate your success. Don't underestimate the power of this theme. Inbound leads will come from these types of posts, your connections will message you, and you will turn your contacts into contracts.

5. Social Proof & Reviews

Have you ever received a gift from a client after doing a great job? What about a text message, email or phone call? What about a hand-written thank you card? Each time you do, it's social proof that you are great at what you do, and also, it's an amazing LinkedIn® post.

We talked about the power of personal recommendations on LinkedIn® earlier; those can also be turned into posts, take a screenshot, and with permission, tag the person who gave you the recommendation. Thank your happy client (tag them with permission) and post the lovely gift, card, text, message etc. and put up a picture of whatever you received. When you have happy customers and others see that you will attract more people towards you.

I regularly receive cards, champagne, flowers, gifts and cards (which is amazing!) from clients who have loved their time on a Masterclass or people that have generated massive results from LinkedIn® as a result of my knowledge. I post about these and share this with my LinkedIn® newsfeed. It brings leads!

Testimonials, reviews, cards, gifts, whatever format they arrive in, you can turn this social proof into great LinkedIn® posts. If you received a review on Facebook, or on Google my business or Amazon, then take a screenshot and post it!

When you demonstrate consistently that your clients appreciate you, then you will build your personal brand and increase the trust with potential clients that you are great at what you do.

6. News Updates

This is an easy theme for salespeople. It's simple. What news do you have about your career, your business, your company, your products, your services, your team? The list goes on. What news can you share that continues to demonstrate that you are busy, growing, doing great things and making things better for your customers. Pick industry related topics to talk about and newsjack where possible and where relevant.

- If you have taken on a new team member, announce it to your LinkedIn® network

- If you have formed a strategic partnership or alliance, announce it

- If you have won an award, share it with your LinkedIn® network

- If you are attending a conference or trade show, announce it to your network

- If you just got a promotion or moved jobs, share it

All of this, as usual, needs to be done in a way that is selling without selling. You will find that people will react to a post like this with comments and the 'Celebrate' reaction on LinkedIn® if you aren't using it as a sales pitch.

7. Ask a Question

This theme could be used across all of the previous seven themes. Asking a question on a LinkedIn® post will drive answers in the comments, which in turn equals engagement.

I was recently training in-house with a corporate sales and marketing team. The UK marketing director was in the training and was excited about heading to London to attend an awards ceremony. He created a post about it in a documentary style which built the credibility of the brand massively due to who they were competing against. He shared what he was up to, i.e. going to London. On its own, it would not have driven a lot of engagement, reactions, yes, but not comments. So I suggested he ask a question.

The question we added to the post was, "What is the best award you have ever won?". Within minutes the post had started to drive a lot of responses, and by the time he left that afternoon, there were more than 20 comments on the post, with people sharing their best award. People love to talk about themselves!

When you ask a question or ask for feedback, your LinkedIn® network will respond. Let's say you are re-branding. You may have a choice of a few different logos or colours to choose from; why not ask your LinkedIn® network to help you decide. Responses will come in the form of comments, and you will drive engagement on your post.

8. Learnings Along the Way

Your journey in your career or your business is going to teach you a great deal. Posts that share what you did and what you learnt, as a result, are great themes for LinkedIn® posts.

It could be about a seminar or event you attended, a book you read, a podcast you learnt from, an interview you watched, or an audible book that you listened to. Maybe you tried something new in your business, and it worked, or you tried something new, and it didn't.

Either way, you are learning all of the time, and by sharing what you did and what you learnt from your experience, you will be adding massive value to your network.

9. Personal Posts

I often get asked about whether you should post about your personal life on LinkedIn®. My view is that there is always a business spin on a personal post. For example, I posted from my holiday in Italy, having stood in the Colosseum in Rome, I created a piece of content about how Rome wasn't built in a day, how important it is to be patient in business and not always seek instant gratification.

I will often post about my kids but linked to their involvement in my business, so Maya has a baking business which she started at age 12, and she has provided cakes and treats for all of our delegates who attend Masterclasses. I post about my passion for kids' enterprise and young entrepreneurship. I posted about how my son Oscar, now 15, learnt how to build a gaming PC from scratch in lockdown.

I post about my role as a Business Ambassador in schools. I post about personal goal setting. I see others post about sporting achievements in their personal life, but linking these back into a business context. So bring your personal life into the LinkedIn® newsfeed to add another angle to you, to increase connection in other ways to your network and add value at the same time.

Human to human, emotional, empathetic posts with a real story to them will always perform well on LinkedIn® especially since lockdown, and don't worry about anyone who comments and says your post belongs on Facebook! Those pesky LinkedIn® 'police' as they are fondly referred to! Personal posts make you human, and people buy from people at the end of the day.

10. Corporate Social Responsibility (CSR)

If you and/or your company are involved in any form of voluntary work, community service or charity involvement, then sharing this on LinkedIn as a post both on your Company page and on your personal profile can help raise visibility both for you, and the organisation or charity that you are supporting.

11. Your Culture

If you have a larger organisation and talent acquisition is high on your agenda, then sharing what it is like to work at your company, what the culture is like, and what the people are like can be a great strategy for attracting new talent. These posts can feature on your personal profile or your Company Page, or both.

12. News Jacking

This is where you jump on a topical theme that is trending in the news. You can see what is trending in the news on LinkedIn® on the home page on the desktop feed and any post that mentions these topics and hashtags will be prioritised by the algorithm. If it's not national news, it could be something happening in your industry that you have an opinion on. You will gain traction quickly from newsjacking when it's done well.

13. Hiring / Recruiting

If you are looking for great talent, have job openings and want to attract great people to your business then posting about your open positions is a content theme you should be using. This content is a great way to rally support from your network and raise awareness about your positions. I cover more about how to use LinkedIn® for recruitment in a later chapter, dedicated to people teams.

14. Dialogue

Easier for salespeople, and this theme is not for everyone. This is where you re-enact a conversation that you have either been a part of, or know is happening in the board room of your prospects, or a conversation you have had with a prospect. These are great for demonstrating your expertise, over-coming objections and addressing the pain points of your IDEAL clients.

15. Ask for Help

The LinkedIn® newsfeed is a supportive place with many knowledgeable and well networked members. If you need help with something, use a post to ask for help. Ask people to tag recommendations in the comments and get suggestions to solve your challenge. You may get in-undated (advance warning), so look for people's names who are being tagged multiple times. You will get high visibility on a post like this.

So that's 15 Content Themes that I recommend for salespeople. If that's not enough and you are still looking for ideas, you can get an additional 100 Content Ideas as a free gift from me and the Pipeline 44 team. Download a PDF with loads of content ideas here:

https://www.pipeline44.com/p/content-ideas

Use this space here to write down your ideas for 3 different LinkedIn® posts for your business now that you have all these ideas:

IDEA 1:

_____

_____

_____

IDEA 2:

_____

_____

IDEA 3:

_____

_____

_____

Now that you have your 15 various themes that salespeople can utilise, let's look at the different styles of posts you can create using images, video, documents, text and more!

There are 14 post types at the time of writing this book, although it can and will change regularly as LinkedIn® introduces new features. To keep it simple, I am only going to talk about the post types that I feel are relevant for salespeople. We'll cover those in the next chapter.

5 ACTIONABLE INSIGHTS FROM THIS CHAPTER

1. Plan out your next 3 posts choosing 3 of the themes mentioned in this chapter.
2. Decide how frequently you want to post, the ideal is 3+ per week, but base this on a frequency you can sustain.
3. Come up with some educational post ideas based on your expertise, tips, helpful answers to questions your prospects would find useful.
4. Look at your diary over the last 7 days, every appointment in your calendar could be a documentary post. Both personal and business related appointments can all be turned into content. What could you document?
5. Go to Answer the public and search on your industry or related topics to what you sell. Look at what questions are being entered into search engines, and come up with some ideas for your content in the future.

Chapter 18
The Best Post Types for Salespeople

This chapter will help you with the actual style of post. We have already looked at the themes which will give you the inspiration for the content itself. Now we will explore how to turn those ideas into actual posts.

There are currently 14 different styles of post that you can use on the LinkedIn® platform to create your content. Not all are relevant for a salesperson, here they all are for reference.

1) Text Only Post
2) Images / Photographs Post
3) Document Post
4) Video Post
5) LinkedIn® Live
6) LinkedIn® Poll
7) LinkedIn® Event
8) LinkedIn® Article
9) LinkedIn® Newsletter
10) LinkedIn® Audio Events
10) Giving Kudos
11) Share that You're Hiring
12) Celebrate an Occasion / Milestone
13) Carousels
14) Using a Template

I will go into more detail on only the ones I believe are suitable for someone building their personal brand, in a sales or sales leadership function.

One thing to bear in mind with all types of posts when you work through these is that the LinkedIn® algorithm looks at something called 'dwell time'. That's the length of time that someone stays on your post, so when you are creating a piece of content, consider the type of post that will work best whilst also considering what will keep people on the post for a longer duration. Dwell time drives impressions, the more impressions (views) you receive on your content, and the more engagement (reactions and comments), the better your post will perform.

Now let's look at each of the post types in more detail. As you read through them, think about how you might apply the ideas you gained in the previous chapter with the post types themselves.

1. Text Posts - Short Form vs. Long Form

When you post on LinkedIn®, only the first three lines of text can be seen; after that, a button called 'See More...' shows up.

A short post will be no longer than three lines. It's a simple piece of text. A long form post makes the 'See More...' button appear. The more people who click on 'See More...' the more views and the more momentum you will create on your post. Make the first three lines count, and use curiosity to get them to click on 'See More...'.

LinkedIn® absolutely LOVES long posts, so keep your short form text posts to a minimum. If you don't have much time, use this style of post, but don't expect it to gain as much visibility as to when you use lots of text. The dwell time (how long someone stays) affects your number of post views.

The same applies when you post photos and videos, you will gain more visibility and views the longer the text that accompanies it. Remember, LinkedIn® likes to keep us as members in LinkedIn®, and the longer your posts are, the longer it takes to read them. This is why you will always get more views, the longer the text on any type of post.

2. Image(s) / Photograph(s) Posts

It is important that your content caters for all different learning styles. Always remember that 70% of LinkedIn® members will prefer visual communication, so posts including photographs and images should be a part of your content strategy.

Images can be those you have taken yourself on your smartphone, or you can use royalty free images. There are some fantastic websites you can use to find great photographs for your posts.
These include: pixabay.com, pexels.com and unsplash.com.

It is important not to use images you find on Google as you could get into issues with copyright. When you use sites that are community led with royalty-free photos, you can search for keywords that represent what you are posting about.
You can post multiple images or a single image on LinkedIn®. The combination that works best is odd numbers, so 1 image, 3 images or 5 images. They just seem to show up better on the mobile newsfeed and desktop versions of LinkedIn® in that combination. I have recently been trialling using 8 photos, and these seem to perform very well as people click on 5+ to see the additional photos, which increases dwell time.

When you add multiple images, you are making a collage effect. You can tag people in your photographs and add stickers to them when you post. I usually try to post at least 2 image posts per week. Often, I will use photos with documentary theme posts, and success/wins themed posts as these seem to work the best with photographs.

3. Document Posts (PDF or PPT)

One of my favourite types of posts and one of the least used! A document post is where you can upload a file such as a PDF or Slide Show in PowerPoint to educate your network on a specific topic. The dwell time on these is HUGE, and I typically see a 3-5 times increase in views on a document post. LinkedIn turns the post into a carousel, and it looks like the turning pages of a book.
Ideas for these types of posts include case studies, white papers, tip sheets, and presentation slides.

The last two document posts I have created have exceeded 25,000 views in both cases, with a lot less engagement and reactions than my normal posts.

If you are going to use document posts, make them highly visual, colourful and simple. Use basic tips and the ideal length of a document would be 12-20 pages or slides.

These are great to use as Educational posts, and LinkedIn loves the interaction with these posts, as people click through page by page to get to the end of the document.

If you have provided value, I would recommend that you have some kind of call to action at the end of the document or a question, to drive further engagement in the comments.

4. Video Posts

Take a moment to pick up your mobile phone. Go to the LinkedIn® app and scroll down the newsfeed to 30-60 seconds. Count how many videos you can see. You will probably get into double figures. Video posts are by far the most engaging and popular on LinkedIn®, especially in a mobile environment. What this tells us is that video HAS to be a part of your content marketing.
Less than 4% of LinkedIn® members are posting video content, so the great thing here is that you can gain a competitive edge and build your personal brand through video whilst it is still relatively under-utilised.

As I mentioned earlier in this chapter, 85% of video content on social media is viewed without sound. Therefore it is important that you include captions on your videos. A great service you can use for this is rev.com. Send your movies off to Rev, and within hours, you will have an SRT file back from them with the transcript of the video. You will pay $1.25 per minute of video on rev.com, and they are 99.8% accurate. When you upload the movie file on LinkedIn®, you can edit the video and simply add the SRT file. Or you can use video editing software such as kapwing.com or iMovie to edit your videos and add in the subtitles.

There are also apps available to help you caption your videos. I love 'Apple Clips' in the Apple Store, or you can use AutoCap if you are on Android, there are plenty of others around too. I like to use these for recording personalised messages to people and then sending video messages, which we spoke about in a previous chapter.

5. LinkedIn® Polls

Polls have been very popular on LinkedIn® since their arrival onto the platform in 2021. There was a period of around 6 months where every other post seemed to be a poll, and everything from basic questions to silly questions and more thought-provoking polls hit the scene, some generating hundreds of thousands of impressions. Everyone loves to express their opinion, and the LinkedIn® algorithm loves them too! If you ask a good quality, engaging poll will still perform well and probably better than some of your other types of posts. Love them or hate them?

I love them for a few reasons…

A) They are easy and quick to post when you are short on time.
B) The answers to the poll can be used to create more content.
C) The visibility on them is crazy! Meaning my poll post reaches far into my 2nd and 3rd degree network, so my personal brand is seen by a lot more people.
D) Interaction with my poll is that person telling the LinkedIn® algorithm that they want to see more from me. So, when I post in the future, my next non-poll post and other content is more likely to show up in their newsfeed. Any poll participant is essentially training the algorithm they want to see more content from you. Which is a hidden element of polls that not many people realise.

So instead of avoiding polls, embrace them! Use them once every couple of weeks to drive your visibility up and learn from your audience.

6. LinkedIn® Events

LinkedIn® Events are a great feature when used correctly. In fact, this is one of the biggest lead generators for our own business. We run a free event for 90 minutes online every month, and we use LinkedIn events to fill it (as well as other marketing techniques). We publish the event 3 weeks in advance of the event, and we put all of the details onto the event and then include a Zoom registration link for people to register that they are attending.

Everyone who expresses interest in attending via the LinkedIn event is a prospect, whether they register on the Zoom link or not. They clearly have a pain we can solve otherwise they would not have expressed interest in attending on the

LinkedIn event page. Each of our team members has the next upcoming LinkedIn event on the featured section of their profile and we take advantage of the 1000 invites each person's profile can use to invite people each week.

If you combine this feature with posting about the event in the newsfeed, featuring the event in your newsletter, building an email list and then the LinkedIn algorithm taking over the promotion of the event as the date gets closer, you can really get some momentum. It may take you a few months to build the audience and secure the numbers that you need, but it's totally worth it when you get the traffic to the event, put on a show that everyone loves, invite people to learn more and then convert attendees into clients.

7. Giving Kudos

This one won't give you lots of impressions, but it will make you feel really good. It's where you get to recognise someone in your network by giving them 'Kudos'. You can pre-select from 8 different types of Kudos, depending on what they have done or achieved. It's a great type of post for team recognition.

When you want to give someone Kudos, simply go to their profile. Use the ellipsis menu (…) which is the same place you go to recommend someone. In the drop-down menu, you have the option to give Kudos. You can also get to this when you create a new post.

8. Share that you're Hiring

Having started out using LinkedIn® as a recruiter, I know how powerful this tool is for finding and attracting great talent. You can create jobs on LinkedIn® when you are hiring and create posts and content to share that you are hiring. You can also refer to the later chapter called 'Social Selling for People Teams'.

9. Celebrate and Occasion / Milestone

This is a relatively simple one. You have the option to post when you start a new role or get a promotion or start a new business. LinkedIn® is a positive community, and the celebration of milestones will usually be well supported on the newsfeed.

Using #Hashtags

Hashtags came on the scene in 2019 on LinkedIn®. When you post your content from the homepage, simply add hashtags using the # symbol. Adding hashtags to your LinkedIn® updates and articles gives them a higher chance of being discovered by LinkedIn® members, who follow or search for the hashtag you've used. If you have Creator Mode switched on, then you will be asked to pick 5 main hashtags that you speak about in your content. Be sure to use these in your posts.

Hashtags can be placed after copy or embedded within the copy on your posts so long as it makes sense to do so. When you post a great piece of content, it can be picked up by the LinkedIn® algorithm, and your post can start trending with that hashtag, which will increase your visibility.

People who you may not even be connected with on LinkedIn® will see the post because they follow that hashtag. I use #socialselling on my posts as one of my main hashtags. I was recently invited to appear on a podcast by an expert in Australia after he found me because I was using #socialselling on my posts. He follows this hashtag because it interests him. We were not connected at all, he wasn't even in my 2nd or 3rd degree network, but he came across me because of the hashtag I was using.

To see how many people are following a LinkedIn® hashtag, enter the hashtag ideas you have for your personal and/or company brand in the main LinkedIn® search bar. The results will show how many members are following that specific hashtag.

Here are some of the most popular hashtags on LinkedIn®.

General

#Mindfulness #Creativity #Leadership #Innovation #Management

#Motivation #Tips #Productivity #Careers #GettingThingsDone

#MentalHealth #Inspiration

Social Media & Marketing

#Branding #KnowYourSocial #SocialNetworking #SocialMedia

#SocialMediaMarketing #SocialMediaAdvertising

#DigitalMarketing #ContentMarketing #OnlineAdvertising

#Marketing #Sales

Small Business & Entrepreneurship

#Business #BusinessIntelligence #SmallBusiness #Entrepreneur

#Entrepreneurship #SocialEntrpreneurship

Like hashtags elsewhere, LinkedIn® hashtags can only include letters, numbers and emojis. Any spaces or symbols used will break the link. That means you cannot use apostrophes, commas, exclamation points, or hyphens. Here are some key punctuation do's and don'ts when it comes to hashtags:
DON'T add spaces. Multiple word hashtags should be grouped together. For example: #JustDoIt not #Just Do It.

DO capitalise multi-word hashtags. TitleCasing will vastly improve readability and will prevent hashtags from being read incorrectly.

DON'T use symbols or punctuation marks. English teachers will cringe over turning I'm into Im or you're into youre, but hashtags operate under their own rules.

DO include punctuation around your hashtag. If your hashtag is in a sentence and should be followed by a comma, end mark, or another form of punctuation, including one will not affect the tag.

DO check your spelling. Hashtags can often be overlooked in proofreads, but a misspelt hashtag is never a good thing.

There are no limits to the number of hashtags you can use in a post on LinkedIn®. That said, I recommend that you limit each post to a maximum of 3-5 hashtags, ideally 3 if you can. Using too many hashtags on LinkedIn® could also result in the LinkedIn® algorithm giving your post less visibility.

LinkedIn® will automatically suggest relevant hashtags when you begin to write a post. If they seem like a good fit, include them. But don't add them just for the sake of it.

Be deliberate in your hashtag use.

Be aware that there is a niche community online for every industry and subject, and they often use specific hashtags. Using the right niche hashtag will connect you to an online community that's passionate about your industry.

Make sure to also check Instagram, Twitter, Reddit or other online forums for inspiration on hashtags.

Start following hashtags relevant to your brand. Posts with the hashtags you decide to follow will show up in your LinkedIn® feed. A list of the hashtags you already follow on LinkedIn® can be found from the homepage in the left sidebar under 'Your communities'.

Click each hashtag to get a glimpse of how others are using them. Look to see if members of LinkedIn® are using additional hashtags that you could be following and using, too.

The company hashtag can be automatically appended to employee posts, which helps to increase the visibility of your company and tag company-related content.

Tagging People in Posts

I have mentioned tagging people a number of times in this chapter; always make sure your tags are relevant. Don't simply tag people because they have a lot of connections (it really annoys me when people do that!).

Always make sure its permission based, or they were an active part of your status update, i.e. that you were with them at an event, you are thanking them personally, or they are in a picture or video you are posting. Simply use the @ symbol and start typing their name in a post with a space in-between their first and last name. The people with that name will show up in a drop-down list. Simply select them, and they will be tagged. Their name will show up bold in either blue or black, depending on which device you are using.

They will be notified that you have tagged them in their notifications, which will encourage them to engage with the post and will ensure that the post is seen by their network as well as yours.

So now you have your 15 content themes and 9 content types that as a salesperson allows you to be completely flexible and never run out of ideas. Remember you can always start with this guide, packed full of 100 content ideas to get you started: http://pipeline44.com/content-ideas

ACTIONS FROM THIS CHAPTER

1. Engage with everyone who comments on your posts, with relevant replies (ideally at least 20 words).

2. Use different content themes for your posts to provide variety to your followers.

3. Use the different types of posts mentioned here to mix up the appeal to different learning styles. Choose one post type you haven't used before and create a post with it.

4. Use hashtags in every post and tag people (if relevant) to get your content found by a wider audience.

5. Always direct your content at your exact IDEAL client, but never, ever sell.

Chapter 19:
Social Selling for Marketing Teams

Most of this book has been dedicated to sales teams and sales leaders. It is critical that any social selling efforts in an organisation, have support and alignment with the marketing department. So marketing, this one's for you!

It is not uncommon for sales and marketing to be misaligned when it comes to lead generation. Sales blaming marketing, for a lack of or poor-quality leads, marketing blaming sales for not following up or doing anything with the data they provide.

Marketing spending time, effort and energy on content creation for the LinkedIn® Company Page and getting frustrated when they ask sales to repost and share it and no-one does. Sound familiar?

Marketing can and should play a huge part in the shaping of the social selling strategy for your organisation. Whenever a sales organisation brings me in to wotrk with them, I always insist that marketing is included in the set up of the strategy and that they also attend the training in full with the sales team to fully understand how sales needs to be supported in their social selling efforts,

The most obvious of ways that Marketing can play a role is through ownership of the LinkedIn® company page. If the company is using them, paid ads will also sit with Marketing, if you are using sponsored or boosted posts in the LinkedIn® environment. Content creation for social media including LinkedIn® usually sits with Marketing. As stewards of your corporate brand, the core message and brand consistency across LinkedIn profiles should be owned by Marketing.

If you are in a Marketing function, go take a look at the LinkedIn profiles of your Leadership Team and sales teams, look at the profiles from a brand perspective, and read them with your marketing hat on. Are you happy that every person in your organisation is meeting brand guidelines, using the right imagery, talking about the business you represent in the right way? There will be a mixture of header images being used, some people will have lovely featured sections helping to promote and market your business and some won't. How many profiles in your company are driving people to your website, to your white papers and case studies. How much traffic is really being driven from LinkedIn® to your website? How many of the sales and Leadership team, as well as other departments are posting consistently, driving brand awareness and creating noise about your Company?

I have mentioned this before, but the personal profiles of the people in your business will get 10 times the reach of the posts you put out on your Company page. Do you know how many followers your company brand has? I don't mean on your Company Page, add up all of the followers of all the people who work for your business. That audience is huge and yet Marketing departments don't usually include that audience in their numbers when they look at metrics and analytics. Let's say you have 250 employees and the average number of followers is 1300, that's 325,000 potential eyeballs on your brand, through post impressions in addition to what you are achieving on the newsfeed on the Company page.

Before we talk about your Company page, I want to really look at how Marketing can support the efforts of the sales team when it comes to social selling.

Make Content Creation Easy for Them

Most salespeople are lazy, or they are not lazy and in most cases are too busy to have time to spend seeking out content from their Marketing team. Create a content vault packed full of videos, images, case studies, customer stories, blogs, articles and information that is easy to access and they can use for creating their own posts on the newsfeed. They want to promote the brand, they want to generate more commission, so make it nice and easy for them to do so.

Support Their Posts

Your Company page can now interact with posts as the Company Page, you can see all employee posts in the Admin section of your Company Page. Like and Comment on the posts of your sales team, both as the Company Page as well as from your own personal profile. This will help both the reach and engagement of their posts. Feature the best ones on your Company Page and tag the person so that they get recognition.

Run Competitions

Run a content competition, the person with the most impressions on a post, the person who gets the most video views. Encourage them to tag the Company Page in their posts to grow the audience of your LinkedIn Company Page. Help them come up with ideas, give them themes to focus their content on. If you have events coming up or you have key dates in the marketing calendar, for product launches or updates, let the sales team know and help them with ideas on how they could creatively put that across the LinkedIn® newsfeeds.

Hashtags

Guide your sales team on which hashtags you want them to use across their social media posts, especially on LinkedIn. I would recommend having one core hashtag that is the main one to use on all posts, and then give them a selection of hashtags to use depending on the content of their post and who it's aimed at.

Social Media Policy

I understand that you need to have one, but don't make it so draconian that they are scared to post anything! Some sales teams are so scared to post anything that they freeze and would rather not, for fear of being disciplined for not following the rules. Obviously, you don't want people to mis-represent the brand, or post religious and political views, but make them feel comfortable to post, to have an opinion to build their own personal brand, to express themselves, in a way that doesn't harm their or your reputation.

Now let's turn our attention to your Company Page.

Your LinkedIn Company Page

Having a Company Page on LinkedIn® is essential. It gives you and your company the opportunity to take part in conversations important to your brand, engage with and grow your audience, and leverage your current employees to spread your brand message. There are 6 key reasons for having a LinkedIn® Company Page:

1. Recruiting & Attracting Great Talent to your Organisation
2. Spreading your Company message through your Employees
3. Raising brand awareness for your Company Brand
4. Promoting your Products & Services
5. Promoting CSR (Corporate Social Responsibility) efforts
6. It's an additional way for you and your Company to be found

If you are reading this and you are in Marketing, it is most likely that you already have someone dedicated to managing the LinkedIn® company page or a team of people if you are part of a larger organisation. You can have multiple page administrators, allowing multiple people from your sales or, in most cases, marketing division to act as the company on LinkedIn®. Company Pages enables you to participate in conversations and respond to comments as the company page.

Content on LinkedIn® Pages

I have already covered a great deal about content in the previous chapters, mostly around what to post to build your personal brand.
The additional types of content to utilise on LinkedIn® pages would be:

- Interviews with Leadership Team Members
- Interviews with staff about what it is like to work for your Company
- Roles you have open and are recruiting for
- Case Studies and White Papers
- Press Releases and Company Updates

- Brand Stories
- Customer Success Stories
- Partner & Channel related news
- Culture, Values, Mission focus
- Behind the Scenes Action
- New Hires, Promotions, Career Moves
- The Story of Your Brand

Once you start creating and sharing content that interests the Followers of your page (your audience), you need to determine whether or not your content strategy is successful.

LinkedIn® Pages now give Admins stronger visual analytics that can be used to further understand your success on the platform. You can filter your dashboard by any time frame to determine how you are performing over time and adjust your strategy accordingly.

All admins will receive a monthly summary email, providing them with the demographics of people visiting the site and which content they are interacting with. You can share the exact same types of posts from LinkedIn® profiles that I covered in earlier chapters, including text, links, photographs, video and documents. The algorithm works in the same way regardless of whether it is a Company page post or a Personal profile post.

Know & Grow your Followers

Your success as a Company brand is tied to your ability to understand your audience. People can 'follow' your LinkedIn® page. The more keyed into the unique challenges, pain points and needs of your audience or followers, the stronger your content will be, and the more it will resonate with your audience. This goes back to what I covered earlier in earlier chapters.

To help you understand exactly what content is resonating with your audience, LinkedIn® Pages offers "Content Suggestions." With content suggestions, simply select your audience, and you'll be presented with a list of topics and articles they are interested in. Create original content based around these topics or share articles your audience is already interested. This update makes it easier than ever to stay active on LinkedIn®, which will drive traffic to your page and increase your follower count. You can filter your dashboard by any time frame to determine how you are performing and adjust your strategy accordingly.

Engage & Empower your Staff

Engagement is just as critical on a company post as it is on a post from your personal profile. The advantage you have as a larger enterprise is that all of your employees can follow your Company LinkedIn® Page and interact, react, and share with their own networks. Imagine having a sales team of 100+ trained on the power of social selling, all sharing updates from your LinkedIn® page. The reach into all their extended networks is massive. Employees generally have ten times the organic reach of a company on LinkedIn®, making them a great resource for expanding your brand's visibility.

Not enough attention is given to how you can leverage your current employees to grow your brand. With the updates to LinkedIn® Pages, admins of your Company page will now receive a notification every time your company is tagged in a post. These posts can easily be shared to your LinkedIn® Page, making it easy to fill your page with content, expand your reach, and humanise your brand. Using your main Company hashtags and encouraging your staff to do the same whenever they post is also key. It is important that your staff (not just sales) are trained effectively on how to act on a platform like LinkedIn®. Social selling is so powerful, when implemented across all employees in the organisation.

Inviting Your Connections to Follow your Page

Invite your connections to follow your LinkedIn® page. This is a significant enhancement and will help to grow followers more quickly. In the admin settings, you can now ask people you are connected with to follow your page. You (and the other admins of the page) can invite 250 a month and you can now filter by location, Company and industry so this can be a targeted activity.

Company Page Completion

It is important that your Company Page is fully completed and 'All Star' just like your personal profiles as mentioned in an earlier chapter. There are some new sections introduced in 2022 that you may not be aware of, so use this list as a checklist to ensure you have everything you need in there to promote your Company and brand effectively, especially if you are hiring.

1. Add a cover image. Click on the **pencil** icon to put your page into edit mode. Now you can upload, reposition or delete the image. The ideal dimensions of your LinkedIn® Page cover image are 1536 X 768 pixels.

2. You can add or edit the rest of your Company Page information by clicking the pencil icon to the right of your company name. Select '**Page info**' in the navigation area on the left, and make your changes to the name, logo and tagline of your LinkedIn® Page.

3. Go to the Overview section on the left to fill in or update your details. Be sure to include a complete company description which is required. Your description must be between 250 and 2,000 characters long, including spaces. As with your LinkedIn® personal profile, I would recommend you to use as many characters as

possible.

4. Include information about your company, your products and services, who you help, and problems that you solve for your clients and always keep your target market, and ideal clients top of mind. Describe your company, and bring in anything unique and credibility building. Anything compelling that will set you apart from your competitors. You may want to mention the key products and services that you provide. I would also recommend including some kind of 'call to action' telling people what you want them to do next.

5. Below this, you can add or edit the information about your company, including your website, phone number, industry, company size, company type and year founded.

6. Now add specialities. You can add up to 20 specialities for your company. These are similar to skills in your personal profile. Think of keywords you want to be found for, reflecting what your company offers.

7. LinkedIn® will ask for 3 hashtags that your Company should be tagged for, choose the 3 most important hashtags and use the tips I gave earlier in Chapter 7 about hashtags to help you select the right ones.

8. Complete the Lead Gen section, a relatively new feature introduced in 2022, you can now add a lead generation form on your Company Page. Ensure you are using this so that you can capture email addresses and / or feed your sales team with leads.

9. Commitments – a new section added late in 2022, you can now include elements about Diversity, Equality and Inclusion (DE&I), Social Impact, Work Life Balance, Sustainability and Career Growth and Learning.

10. Workplace – You can also now include information about your workplace in terms of policies around remote, hybrid and office working. All introduced post-Covid. It's worth checking to make sure your Company page is fully completed and up to date with this information.

Analytics

Familiarise yourself with all the reports and stats available to you as a Company Page owner or manager. On the homepage of your Company page, you will see key metrics on the left-hand side, track these on a consistent basis and set realistic targets for your page growth.

Marketing has a vital role to play in the social selling strategy of your organisation. If you are reading this and you are in a sales leadership function, talk to your marketing department. See how you can align and work together to improve your effectiveness in the LinkedIn® environment.

If you are in a Marketing function, I run training and consultancy sessions with Marketing teams to help everyone in the marketing department with LinkedIn and Social Selling strategy, if this is something you would be interested in exploring then drop me a message on LinkedIn® or send an email to hello@pipeline44.com.

5 ACTIONABLE INSIGHTS FROM THIS CHAPTER

1. If you are in sales, ensure that your peers in the marketing team read both 'Linked Inbound' and this book 'Linked Outbound'. If you are in marketing, ensure that your peers in sales leadership read this book, as well as 'Linked Inbound'.

2. Work out how many real followers your company has on LinkedIn®, look at how many followers each employee has and imagine the impact of brand amplification if each was empowered to own their own personal brand and post on the newsfeed.

3. Review your Company Page on LinkedIn®. Look at how much your employees are interacting and supporting your posts.

4. Check all aspects of your Company Page, to ensure it is giving you and your Company the best chance of success.

5. Ensure you are supporting your sales teams, arming them with content, case studies, social proof, videos, images and more that they can use as they build their personal brand. Empower them to own their own personal brand, posting a combination of company focused posts but primarily focused on sharing their own original posts based on the content themes in this book.

Chapter 20:
Social Selling for Leadership Teams

Are you a Dinosaur, Doubter, Dabbler or Doer?

I was looking back on my notes from my very first client briefing, ahead of stepping into a Corporate boardroom full of Senior Executives in Paris. I was going there to train a room full of Leaders from across Europe on the power of Social Selling and the importance of them owning their personal brand, positioning themselves as a Thought Leader in their industry on LinkedIn.

"Sam, let me tell you, you are walking into a room mainly of full of Dinosaurs and Doubters. You've got your work cut out!" said the Commercial Director for Europe at the time.

It got me thinking, and since then I have identified 4 types of Leaders when it comes to Social Selling.

The Dinosaurs ☐

Leaders that think that LinkedIn is some platform for jobs, they don't have a profile or if they do it's not been touched for years, their photo is usually 15 years old, they have never posted any content or engaged with the newsfeed. They believe that social media is not going to help the business grow and is a 'total waste of time' for them and their sales team, it's just one big distraction. They don't get it, they don't understand it and are in many cases fearful of it.

The Doubters ☐

Leaders that are highly skeptical of social media, social selling and platforms like LinkedIn. They have every right to be doubtful, they've never seen it work! Their sales, marketing and recruitment team seem to spend hours on LinkedIn but don't get any results.

They don't see the point in investing time and energy into something because there is very little tangible revenue coming into their sales pipeline from the company wide efforts. They simply don't believe in the power of LinkedIn & Social Selling but are open to having their minds changed.

The Dabblers ☐

The leaders who are giving it a go. They are dabbling in social media, they have heard that putting themselves out there might be a good thing to do, they have seen other leaders they know in other companies and from their competitors building their brand, posting content on LinkedIn, and think well maybe I should have a go too. Their version of 'dabbling' is showing a bit of support to their marketing and recruitment teams. Re-sharing the rubbish that is being posted on the company page, or posting the latest jobs they are hiring for, but very rarely sharing their opinion or coming up with anything original. At least they are having a go...

The Doers □ □

The Doers are a rare breed. These are the Corporate Leaders who clearly understand the power of their personal brand. They are thought leaders, they are out there, owning it, sharing original and powerful messages with their networks. They are helping their business to attract great talent, they are positioning themselves and the brand they represent as a market leader.

They are posting consistently, they are regularly engaging with their network, they are responsive. The Doers understand that by being visible and credible on LinkedIn and other platforms, that they are helping to build relationships with customers, partners, their employees, their next best hire and their peers. The Doers get it. They understand the power of Thought Leadership, Personal Brand and Social Selling, they embrace it for themselves, and they embed and enable it across their entire organisations.

So which are you, a Dinosaur, Doubter, Dabbler or Doer? Which of these do you recognise in your own boardroom? If you are an employee are you proud of how your leaders show up online? If you are looking to work for an organisation do you check out the profiles of the leadership team?

Leadership Teams and Boards of Directors who understand the power of social selling leverage their audience, their following, their expertise and their personal brand to give significant reach to their organisation.

As of August 2022, these are some of the most followed business leaders on LinkedIn®:

Bill Gates   36.2 million followers
Richard Branson   19.8 million followers
Jeff Weiner   10.7 million followers
Melinda Gates   7.2 million followers
Simon Sinek   6.4 million followers
Adam Grant   4.9 million followers
Brigette Hyacinth 4.3 million followers
Liz Ryan   3.1 million followers

I was interviewed on a the 'Connected Leadership' podcast hosted by Andy Lopata, with a mutual client, Phil Jones MBE of Brother UK. If I were to get to you to follow anyone in the UK who has personal branding on LinkedIn® set up well from a Leadership standpoint, it would be Phil.

Here is a link to my interview where I was a guest on the show and we explored his personal brand and take on how vital it is to do this as a Leader in business: https://youtu.be/OlDNRcH21tY.

Building a Personal Brand – Where to Start?

So, you've decided to step out of the shadows and build your personal brand but where do you start? Here are some questions that will help you to figure this out:

- What do you want to be known for?
- What topics do you feel strongly about?
- What are your top 10 areas of knowledge and expertise
- What have you got to say that others would resonate with?
- Who do you want to inspire?
- Who has heavily influenced you in your career?
- What other personal brands do you admire in business?
- What are your core values as a person
- What are your core values as a business
- What mission are you on and how can your brand support this?
- What do you feel most opinionated about?
- What have been your greatest lessons in life?
- What have been your greatest lessons in business?

All of these answers can and will shape your personal brand. This is also all great content! Think about why you want to build your personal brand and who you will inspire and influence in the process. If you are a Leader you have a big weight of responsibility on your shoulders, to your staff, your family, your peers, your shareholders, key stakeholders, to your industry. If you choose to build your brand and have a voice on the newsfeed, be clear about why you are doing it and understand how much it can truly help others in the process.

The main message for you if personal branding and thought leadership is new to you, is just to start. Your opinion counts, your company needs you to step up. I know you have a lot to give. Start with a couple of posts a week, look at what other leaders are doing both inside and outside of your organisation. If you are stuck, have someone from your team interview you and ask you questions to get all that expertise out of your head. Brainstorm all the things you know, all the things you are good at, all of the lessons you could pass on to others. The most important thing is to be authentically YOU!

ACTIONS FROM THIS CHAPTER

1. Look at the LinkedIn profiles of yourself and the other Leaders in your Company. What type of Leaders do you identify in the boardroom of your organisation? Dinosaurs, Dabblers, Doers or Doubters?

2. Look at how much you or your Leadership Team is showing up on LinkedIn®, what content are you/they sharing, how visible are you/hey? How much are they engaging with the posts from your organisation and team?

3. If you are a Leader reading this, take a serious look at how you are showing up. How could you do a better job of social selling in your role? You are a thought leader; you are an industry expert. You can help your entire organisation to attract new talent, build better relationships, be more visible to channel, customers, suppliers and support your teams. Think about your personal brand and how you could leverage it.

4. Gift a copy of this book to your Leadership Team if they are open to it.

5. Watch the interview with myself, Phil Jones MBE of Brother UK and Andy Lopata: https://youtu.be/OlDNRcH21tY.

Chapter 21:
Social Selling for People Teams

Having spent 14 years in recruitment, I feel uniquely qualified as a LinkedIn® Expert to help people teams. Finding strong candidates to fill roles is challenging at the best of times, post-Covid the fight for talent is harder than ever. The good news is, there is a lot that can be done from an Employer Branding perspective, as well as using LinkedIn® proactively to search for, approach and attract the best talent to your business.

Whether you are reading this as a hiring manager, a business owner or as a member of a HR department in a larger organisation, my aim for this chapter is to give you smart ways to think outside the box when it comes to attracting great talent.

Most companies approach recruitment for existing positions like this…

1) Someone unexpectedly hands in their notice.
2) Panic sets in by hiring manager.
3) Speak to HR. Create job description.
4) Start advertising on job boards, LinkedIn® and on careers section of company website.
5) Hope and wait for the perfect candidate to drop into the inbox.
6) Get some CV's, mostly not matching the role.
7) Interview unsuccessfully.
8) Weeks pass by, role still not filled, company objectives not being met.
9) Eventually find someone, with a notice period of 2-3 months.
10) Months go by with the role open, the new hire finally starts.
11) Someone else has left the team, unexpectedly and the cycle starts again.

Sound familiar? The week I was writing this chapter, I was speaking with a Senior Sales Manager in a large hardware company. He has been recruiting a Key Account Representative for his sales team for almost 2 years!! He has tried everything, job boards, recruitment agencies, careers website, LinkedIn® and nothing! We were talking about the concept of 'Build the Bench'.

Build the Bench

Imagine having a never-ending stream of great candidates, on tap, at all times, who have been pre-qualified, want to work for your Company and are on stand-by should a new position become available.

When you implement the 'build the bench' methodology, using social selling you can approach passive candidates (i.e.

those currently not looking for a new position) and start conversations with amazing talent that are open to exploring career opportunities with you and your team.

This will be a relatively new concept to your HR department who traditionally rely on advertising roles and agencies only when a position is open. Combine build the bench with employer branding and talent attraction and your recruitment headaches go away.

At the Pipeline 44 agency, we run 'Build the Bench' campaigns across the world for companies who are regularly hiring great people. It's a great solution for scale-ups and businesses experiencing massive growth who need lots of the same type of role quickly. It's also a good idea for companies who experience attrition and typically take months or years to fill their open positions.

Whether you decide to build the bench as a hiring manager, have someone internally do this for you whether you decide to outsource this function, if you are not building the bench, you are losing money. Every day that role is open, your company is not meeting its objectives, especially if that role is a critical position and/or a sales function.

Imagine a sports team, the subs bench is always full of great talent ready to step in if one of the players gets injured and can no longer participate in the game. Within seconds the next player is on the pitch. Build the bench, from a recruitment perspective, is bit like that, although it may take a bit longer for the candidate to step into play.

So How Does It Work?

Firstly, you need to identify the roles and departments in your organisation that could benefit from a build the bench approach. Some of these departments, in fact most of them, won't necessarily have a current open vacancy to fill. Look at where the flight risks are, look at the departments and people who you know, if they handed their notice in tomorrow, would leave your business with a short-term problem.

Once you've identified the roles, decide who is going to take on this activity. I personally don't recommend that it is a recruitment agency or someone in your HR team. This works best coming from the hiring manager. A passive candidate is more likely to connect with a peer in a similar industry, especially if you are with a well-known or up and coming brand.

I recommend using Sales Navigator™ for any build the bench work.

Use Sales Navigator™ to identify companies who match the places you want to recruit passive candidates from. Use the IDEAL client template from a previous chapter if it helps. Then build 'Account Lists' within Sales Navigator™ so you can put together a hit list of the companies you want to headhunt people from.

Once you have your 'Account List' you can build a 'Leads List' in Sales Navigator™ full of the people who match your job description on paper. Ensure you include in your Boolean search and your filters, all of the keywords, skills and experience you want your potential next hires to have.

I recommend approaching 100-200 potential candidates a month, so you will need 200-400 people in your lists for a month's worth of building the bench (based on a 50% conversion of candidate approach to acceptance.

Your 1st message, the invitation to connect, should use the principles talked about in earlier chapters. Making it as personalised as possible and not mentioning the reason for you inviting them to connect.

Your 2nd message, the follow up once connected, should focus on the fact that you don't currently have an open position, and find out if they are 'open' to a confidential chat about future career opportunities with your company. From every 100 candidate approaches, you will find that 20-25 are likely to respond. Some positive and some negative. The ones who aren't interested are great sources for referrals. If they are not looking, they may know someone who is.

The ones who are positive and open to a chat, invite them to send over their CV and offer them an initial 15 mins confidential conversation.

For every 100 approaches you should end up with 5-10 who are serious, open to a chat, who send their CV and want to speak to you. Do this every month consistently, that's 60-120 candidates every year. 1-5% of these will be A-star talent, as in perfect for the role, super talented and you want them in your team yesterday! You won't always get them, but they are the hot ones on your list. Move them to a new 'A Star' list in Sales Navigator™ and nurture them. Check in regularly, and when you have an open position get ready to move on them. Keep them updated, keep the conversation going and express genuine interest in them and their career.

Then you will have others, the B's the ones that you want to take forward to interview, the minute that a role becomes available. Usually this is the next 20-25%. That's a strong pool of talent who you already know have a good fit for the role, you've spoken to already and you would be happy to move them through the recruitment process as and when something becomes available. You already have their CV's, you will have found out some basic information in your initial chat to learn more about them and more importantly they know about you and your company. They will have researched the Company and the leadership team, hence why it's so important for everyone in the business to play a part in social selling.

So the A's and B's are warmed up and now you have a pool of people to go to as soon as a position is open. Some will have been promoted, some will have received a pay rise, some will have gone from 'I'm happy where I am' to 'actually I'm not happy anymore', I'm more open now.

Circumstances change all the time in companies and people's careers, but if you are in touch, nurturing the relationship and they continue to see you on the newsfeed, you and your team and your brand are staying top of mind.

You can keep lists of all candidates, make notes on them and when you either have budget to increase your team's headcount or one of your current team leaves, you are prepared. You are proactive and you can move quickly.

Most of this book is about filling your sales pipeline, but your talent pipeline is just as important if you want to grow your business with great people.

Are you building your bench? Do you know what you would do if your best person handed in their notice tomorrow? How much money is your company wasting on recruitment agencies and job boards?

The fight for talent is real. Building the bench is not a nice idea, it's a 'must do', if you want to build a team with the best people and beat your competitors.

ACTIONS FROM THIS CHAPTER

1. Look at the roles in your organisation that a 'Build the Bench' approach would be suitable for.

2. Build a list of key industries and key accounts (companies) you would love to target people from, inside Sales Navigator™.

3. Build a list of Leads (people) that fit the job roles you have identified inside Sales Navigator™.

4. Construct your Message 1 (invitation), Message 2 (follow-up) and Message 3 (response) for each candidate type.

5. Nurture your lists, get organised and start collecting CV's and building relationships with amazing talent so you are ready and prepared to fill the next vacancy.

Chapter 22:
Habits and Systems for Success

The key to success with any form of social selling on any platform is consistency. Your LinkedIn® SSI can go up just as quickly as it can go down. LinkedIn® membership is like a gym membership, you've actually got to go to the gym, listen to the instructors, follow a system, use the equipment and be consistent to get any kind of results.

It's the same with LinkedIn®, you need to be active on LinkedIn® daily, not just when you feel like it. You need to show up, be there, engage with people in your network, build relationships, deliver great content and be consistent with your outreach to prospects for it to actually work.

Don't expect instant results, it could happen but it's more likely that it will be 3-6 months of implementation before you start to see things change. Why? Because it takes time to build up your personal brand, it takes time to grow your visibility and increase your credibility. It takes patience and consistency to build up a network of prospects in your exact target market, and then with some testing and trialling different approaches it's going to take some time before you start to get regular responses to your outreach.

However, if you do apply the daily, weekly and monthly habits I am going to give you in this chapter, CONSISTENTLY, you will start to see results.

So let's look at planning for success, and that starts with habits. There are a couple of great books on this topic, my favourite being 'The Power of Habit' by Charles Duhigg. So I won't even attempt to educate you on this topic, he does a much better job than me.

I have designed these habits for you to be able to achieve them in as little time as possible, from just 20 minutes a day. If you choose to spend more time then you will supercharge your results.

I am a believer that what gets scheduled, gets done! It is very important to block out time in your calendar each day, week and month to ensure that these tasks happen.

5 Daily Habits

Each day here are the key things to focus on, all of which will help you drive up your LinkedIn® Social Selling Index (SSI), in just 20 minutes a day:

1) Log in to LinkedIn® either on your desktop or on the mobile app

2) Check your inbox for new messages and respond (2-5 minutes)

3)   Create one post, in line with the content strategies shared in this book

4)   Like, Comment and/or Share others posts from within your network. Engage with their content and engage with or create discussions on others posts (1-3 minutes)

5)   Run a Boolean search and find 10 prospects in your target market, send them a personalised connection request. (10 minutes)

5 Weekly Habits

Each week here are the key things to focus on, all of which will help you to drive up your LinkedIn® Social Selling Index, in just 30 mins a week:

1.   Give a recommendation to someone else in your 1st degree network (3 mins)

2.   Check your Social Selling Index (SSI) overall score and track it (2 mins)

3.   Go through your inbox and respond to all people who have accepted your connection request, then send your chosen follow up 2nd message (15 mins)

4.   Track your conversion rate of invitation to acceptance (ideally this should be somewhere between 50-70%) (5 minutes)

5.   Track your conversion rate of 2nd message to positive response (ideally this should be between 3-8%) (5 minutes)

4 Monthly Habits

Each month here are the key things to focus on, all of which will help you to drive up your LinkedIn® Social Selling Index, in just 1-2 hours a month:

1.   Back up your data by downloading a copy of your connections. (2 Mins)

2.   Check all your LinkedIn® statistics and track them including profile views, search appearances, average post views, SSI trends

3.   Build your People and Account lists in Sales Navigator – set yourself up for success (2 hours)

As with anything new, where consistency is required, it's always good to have an accountability partner. Why not share this book with a close friend, colleague, business partner, client or contact and ask them to be your accountability partner?

Ideally pick someone who is highly competitive and challenge them to an SSI race! Run a 90 Day Challenge to see who can create the highest SSI, that way you can be sure that you will be implementing your habits and have some fun at the same time!

5 ACTIONABLE INSIGHTS FROM THIS CHAPTER

1. Decide how much time you will dedicate to LinkedIn each day.

2. Plan in your LinkedIn time into your diary (I find first thing easiest)

3. Map out your daily, weekly and monthly habits.

4. Set yourself up for success, track all your activities.

5. Commit to a consistent run of 90 days. Decide. Commit. Succeed.

Chapter 23:
Actions and Next Steps

Congratulations! You made it to the final chapter. Thank you, I know it's a LOT of information! I have put together some thoughts on where you go from here whether you choose to go it alone or together.

Create your Social Selling Strategy

Decide which elements of this book you are going to implement. Look at what is most relevant for you, your business and your team. Spend some time digesting everything and going through the actions after each chapter.

Look at who else in your organisation needs to read this book. You now have all this knowledge. Does someone in your leadership team, marketing team or sales team need to read it? This book, and my previous book "Linked Inbound" can be purchased in bulk from me directly, so drop me a message on LinkedIn if you want to order more than 20 books at a time.

Make your plan, then decide if you are going to go it alone or bring in professional help. If you are going to bring in professional help, then be sure to read my Article on the '10 things to look for before hiring a LinkedIn and Social Selling expert'.

I won't be offended if it's not me, but I want you to choose well.

10 Things to Look For When Hiring a LinkedIn® & Social Selling Expert

Bespoke Corporate Training & Consultancy (Large Teams)

If you decide after reading this, that you want to bring me and the Pipeline 44 team into your organisation to work with you, then the best next step would be to book in a discovery call with us, to see if we are a good fit for each other. You can book a call using this link:

http://calendly.com/samrathling/strategycall

Examples of recent bespoke corporate training we have undertaken:

- Bespoke deep-dive Sales Navigator training for Sales Teams
- 3 year Social Selling roll out across 23 European countries, with 50 Marketing professionals, 180 Salespeople and 20 Senior Leadership Team members in the Computer Hardware industry
- A 12-month programme to roll out Social Selling through a global sales team of 200 employees in the Print industry.
- Deep-dive Sales Navigator training for Sales Teams (in-house and online)

- 2 Day in-house Social Selling Masterclass for all Sales and Marketing Teams.
- Company Pages Training and Consultancy
- Leadership Team: Thought Leadership & Personal Branding on LinkedIn®

Every organisation is different and has varying needs. It's not a one size fits all. So do get in touch with me to explore what solution is right for you and your team. Email: hello@pipeline44.com or message me directly on LinkedIn®.

Sales Navigator Masterclasses (Small Teams & Individuals)

In September 2022, due to popular demand, I started running public Sales Navigator Masterclasses. These run 8 times a year via online Zoom sessions to cater for all geographies. The course runs over 6 weeks at lunchtimes UK time, on the same day and time each week consecutively. You will learn with me for 90 mins a week and get to implement everything that you need to know about LinkedIn®, Social Selling and Sales Navigator™. We will work on your profile, we will come up with your prospecting messages together, you will leave with a complete content plan, a proper social selling strategy and all the skills you need to build sales pipeline from LinkedIn®.

You can book your ticket to the next Sales Navigator Masterclass here: http://pipeline44.com/masterclass

You can learn more on this Smart Link □:
https://www.linkedin.com/smart-links/AQFWspzTYrFlkQ

This is suitable for small sales teams (up to 10 salespeople from one organisation) as well as individual business owners, and sales professionals who want to pay to attend themselves or get it funded by their organisation. These usually sell out in advance and capacity is 20 delegates per class.

Pipeline 44 Social Selling Academy (For Small Business)

Everything we know about social selling and LinkedIn® has been captured in the most comprehensive digital marketing, social selling and LinkedIn® training on the planet. This is both online education as well as ongoing accountability and support. We run weekly group coaching sessions for all Academy members, to keep you focused on implementation. We have a vibrant community in our Slack channel, dedicated to helping and supporting our members. Questions come in daily, and we support everyone in our community throughout each month at every stage of their journey. Become a part of a community of like-minded people on their own social selling journey and get your questions answered.

Learn at your own pace and work with me for a minimum 12 months to learn and implement everything I know about how to generate business from LinkedIn®. The Academy is accessible to everyone, whether you are starting out, in a sales function or an experienced business owner. Get yourself trained, get your team trained.

Many of our corporate clients create their own bespoke version of the Academy, giving their sales and marketing teams access to me and all of the content so that they can learn what they need to in order to generate results from LinkedIn® and social selling.

With a full module dedicated to Sales Navigator™ there really is no other training like it for both beginners and more advanced LinkedIn® users. We have members from across the globe and every month, our clients who implement with consistency and focus secure more leads, more business and new opportunities from what they are learning.

Learn more or become a member here: http://pipeline44.com/academy

With prices starting from just £150 a month per person*, you can access me and my team to help you on your social selling journey. (Note: *price subject to change)

'Done with You' Solutions

It's easy to read a book like this and get totally overwhelmed. You might be thinking, I can't possibly see how I am ever going to have the time to do it all. Others see the value in working with a team of highly trained experts who can support them in their efforts.

Pipeline 44 Group is a company who trains and educates SME's and Corporates on social selling through LinkedIn®, but we also have dedicated campaign teams who you can outsource elements of your social selling work to.

In one of the earlier chapters of this book, I outlined the 8 different ways to prospect, the different types of campaigns. We provide LinkedIn® marketing campaigns to support each one of those. To remind you, the campaign types are:

- Network Building Only (sending 1st messages only)
- Brand Building Only (putting out content for you, no prospecting)
- Prospecting for Talent (building the bench with 100 candidates a month)
- Relationship Building (starting conversations with your IDEAL client)
- Fill Your Events (helping you to fill online and offline events with prospects)
- Starting Sales Conversations (PAIN Killer Formula)
- Added Value Give Away (helping you to get in front of more prospects)
- Key Account Targeting (targeted efforts for Enterprise B2B)

Regardless of the campaign type you think could suit your business, the best next step would be to book in a call so we can understand your business more and talk through the options. Each campaign type is priced differently, with a minimum 6 months commitment.

Content can also be done with you as well as prospecting, we can look at doing both with you. We are selective about who we take into the agency so when we speak, we will be able to assess if we are a good fit for each other.

Book a call for our 'done with you' solutions.
http://calendly.com/pipeline44/discovery

Access to the Pipeline 44 Academy is mandatory if you become an agency client. You need to commit to both learning and educating yourself along the way as well as our team helping with certain elements, otherwise it simply won't work.

Other Ways to Learn More From Sam Rathling

LinkedIn Newsletter

You can subscribe to my LinkedIn newsletter "Rathling's Ramblings" using this link:

https://www.linkedin.com/newsletters/6730083353548070912/

Social Selling with Sam Podcast

You can subscribe to my 'Social Selling with Sam' podcast here:
https://podfollow.com/1578227493

Depending on whether you are on a desktop or mobile this should direct you to the right version of the podcast for your device.

YouTube Channel

You can subscribe to my YouTube channel here:
https://youtube.com/samrathling

2023 is the year of me getting my YouTube channel sorted! So if you look now and there's not much there, watch this space!

Follow Sam on Social Media:

LinkedIn: https://www.linkedin.com/in/samrathling-linkedinexpert/
Instagram: https://instagram.com/samrathling
TikTok: https://www.tiktok.com/@samantharathling/
Pipeline 44 Group: https://linkedin.com/company/72732937/

About the Author Sam Rathling

Sam is Founder and Chief Revenue Officer (CRO) of the Pipeline 44 Group. Sam is best known for her ability to transform the sales pipeline of her clients. An early adopter of LinkedIn® having spent 14 years in the recruitment industry, Sam has been sharing her knowledge of LinkedIn® and Social Selling since 2010.

In 2021 Yahoo! Finance named her as a Top 10 Global LinkedIn® Expert to follow and she is globally recognised as a leading trainer for corporate and multi-national clients, one of only a handful of LinkedIn experts globally who is truly specialised in Sales Navigator™.

In her role as a social selling strategist, she works with both Corporates & SME's delivering training, mentoring and knowledge transfer programmes. As well as writing this book, she is best-selling Author of 'Linked Inbound' which has already received over 200 five-star reviews. Her podcast 'Social Selling with Sam' sits in the top 5% globally of most downloaded podcasts.

Sam's methodologies have generated in excess of £140m in new revenue for her clients, this number goes up every month as our client's close new business all the time. With over 295 recommendations on LinkedIn® she is a trusted authority, a real expert in her field. An award-winning business owner, a Mum to 3 amazing children, Sam is mentored by some of the most successful business people in the UK, and when not working, loves to spend time in her home from home, the Algarve in Portugal (where most of this book was written). Connect with Sam on LinkedIn via her profile here: Sam's LinkedIn Profile

133

Printed in Great Britain
by Amazon

27802944R00076